: perfor

Finding, Hiring, and Keeping Peak Performers

Finding, Hiring, and Keeping Peak Performers

EVERY MANAGER'S GUIDE

Harry E. Chambers

PERSEUS PUBLISHING
Cambridge, Massachusetts

Copyright © 2001 by Harry E. Chambers
Cataloging-in-Publication card is available from the Library of Congress.
ISBN: 0–7382–0289–4

Perseus Publishing is a member of the Perseus Books Group.
Visit us on the World Wide Web at www.perseuspublishing.com.

Perseus Publishing books are available at special discounts for bulk purchases in the U.S. by corporations, institutions, and other organizations. For more information, please contact the Special Markets Department at the Perseus Books Group, 11 Cambridge Center, Cambridge, MA 02142, or call 617-252-5298.

Text design by Tonya Hahn
Set in 10.5-point Janson by Perseus Publishing Services

First printing, April 2001
1 2 3 4 5 6 7 8 9 10—03 02 01

To Chris,
Patrick,
Mike and Sandy,
Shari and Eddie,
and to the newest member of our family,
Andrew Harrison Harper

Contents

Part III   Keeping Peak Performers

Acknowledgments

This book was written because of the increasing importance for every manager in America to find, hire, and keep peak-performing employees. Many factors have converged to make this challenge evermore important and difficult. It has become one of the core responsibilities of frontline managers, and, in many cases, it can be the most critical factor determining success or failure.

I would like to thank those who participated in the creation of this book. They were kind enough to share their time and intellect. Their contributions were invaluable; without them, this book would be incomplete.

First and foremost, I would like to thank my wife, Chris, for her support, dedication, and editing prowess. She has the ability to tell me when certain segments require more work without doing significant damage to my ego. She also has the ability to edit the material and increase its readability. This book is a microcosm of my life; I couldn't do any of it without her.

Once again, Mickey Beatty, was extremely dedicated in her help and support in creating the manuscript. Her flexibility in accommodating my schedule and deadline demands was extremely valuable, and as always with Mickey, she was there when I needed her. I continue to be amazed at her ability to take my disjointed thoughts and scribblings and forge them into a coherent message. And I know she reads at least one foreign language—mine! Mickey and her husband, Mike, have become valuable friends, and they are among the special people of my life.

I would also like to acknowledge the people who helped me to develop my hiring and recruiting skills during my business career. Roger Morin and Dr. Morris Spear were the early teachers whom I was fortunate to learn from. Much of my success in life can in some measure be traced back to them. They helped teach me the initial skills that were sharpened by many years of experience.

I would also like to thank the people who actively participated in providing background and attributable information for this book; they were very generous with their time and very open in sharing their expertise. Tom Trotter, Howmet Castings; Chuck Coker, Life Stride Performance Systems; Terry Luck, Nationwide Advertising Service; Butch Krishnamurti and John Korzec, Otis Elevator Company; Art Lucas, Cheryl Anderson, and Mike Devereaux of The Lucas Group; and Hunter Johnson, World Strides. All contributed information of great value. They are among the extremely talented men and women who make the American workplace work.

I was also very fortunate to be able to work once again with Julie Stillman, who has to be the greatest and most patient editor on the planet. Nick Philipson of Perseus Books was also very supportive, and I thank him and all the editorial people at Perseus for their kindness in giving me another opportunity to write.

This book is not written from a theoretical or extensively researched point of view. It is based, as is all of my work, on real-world workplace experience. It is targeted specifically toward the men and women who are in frontline and middle management and responsible for the productivity of others.

PART ONE

Finding Peak Performers

Realities, Challenges, and Hiring Traps in Today's Workplace

As a frontline manager, you are faced with an unprecedented number of challenges. Your responsibilities are increasing, and the speed at which you are held accountable for your decisions and the productivity of your people is escalating at a pace unparalleled in either organizational or economic history. You are required to do more with less, and you may even be asked to manage functions and processes about which you have little experience or firsthand knowledge. The demand to meet increasingly tougher standards of time, costs, and quality intensify with each passing day, and your goals and objectives are constantly changing. Your responsibilities are being redefined faster than you can figure out what you are being asked to do. Even the smallest tasks seem to bear a tremendous weight of urgency; failure to stay focused on your critical activities brings negative consequences that not only affect your career, but the productivity and careers of many others.

Few of your responsibilities are as important or as consequential as finding, hiring, and keeping peak-performing employees. You live and die professionally on the performance of your people. You would be hard-pressed to identify many other decisions that have a greater influence on your career and your organization's overall success than those of employee selection and longevity. Yet, as important as these decisions are, you have probably received little or no training in the skills necessary to accomplish them successfully. Your current level of competency is more likely a tribute to your perseverance in trial and error rather than the guidance, training, or mentoring you have received to enhance your skills.

This book was written to provide you, the frontline manager, with the real-world tools you need to increase your ability to find, hire, and keep peak-performing employees. You will not find a lot of theory or academically driven processes to program your behavior. You will find experience-based skills and strategies to help you find and keep the people who will have a positive impact on your productivity and, frankly, increase your value as a manager.

This book is not necessarily written for the human resources professional who is immersed in the activities associated with hiring employees; it is focused on the frontline manager who makes specific, perhaps infrequent, hiring decisions and has a great personal stake in the outcomes of these decisions.

Throughout this book you will find real-world comments and recommendations from savvy business professionals who excel in the skills of hiring and retention. Some are top-notch human resources professionals, some are managers who are accountable for the day-to-day success of their organizations, and some are specialists with unique backgrounds and experiences. All are grounded in the real-world challenges of today's workplace. They are realists, not theorists.

Increasing your skill in hiring and retention will have a major influence on almost everything you do as a manager; it is a responsibility too important to be left to chance, yet many frontline managers make untrained, instinctive decisions under excruciating time pressures. Activities and decisions whose outcomes are too important to allow significant margins for error are conducted under conditions that create huge potential for unacceptable probabilities of error.

Realities

Various complex and significant real-world challenges affect your hiring and retention efforts in today's workplace. Perhaps chief among them, unfortunately, is that the managerial skills of recruiting, interviewing, people development, and leadership that are necessary to retain people and keep employees performing at exceptional levels are among the least-developed skills in the workplace. Many managers have been trained for and have acquired great experience in the technical aspects of their responsibilities, yet the people skills or intrinsic components of their jobs remain unaddressed. The skills you have developed in these areas were probably learned the hard way through on-the-job training.

Human resources professionals usually receive adequate training in hiring and interviewing; frontline managers, supervisors, department heads, team leaders, and most executives do not. When training is provided, in many cases it is not designed to increase your hiring and management effectiveness. It is focused defensively, intended to raise your awareness of legal issues and to protect the organization from liability and lawsuits. Usually, this type of training is mandatory, perfunctory, and designed to protect the organization's financial assets. It provides the documentation showing that you were trained and it is not the organization's fault if you don't do it properly!

Such training is not intended to help you in developing people and performance skills.

Lack of training extracts an extremely high price from your organization and from your career development.

Another real-world truth is that the best way to avoid employee behavior and performance problems is not to hire people with these problems in the first place. One of the best ways to accomplish positive organizational productivity and growth is to hire excellence. Unfortunately, as critical as the hiring and retention function is, many frontline managers rely on instinct or gut level hunches for their hiring decisions. What other options do you have when you have never been taught to do it differently? Some managers even con themselves into believing that instinct is an effective selection strategy. You may hear such statements as "I can look someone in the eyes and tell whether they're lying to me or whether they're going to do a good job." Hiring by psychic power and relying on instinct and hunch is a deadly and costly managerial behavior. Because you have achieved the level of vice president, department head, supervisor, or team leader does not automatically guarantee that you have the skills to identify talent and ability or to interview, recruit, and retain highly productive people.

The reality also exists that many candidates are becoming highly skilled and practiced in the interviewing and hiring process. Frequently they receive specific training on how to interview, and they may have extensive experience in the process. As more people use short-term vision when looking at employment opportunities on the assumption they will soon be moving on, they become more experienced in the skills of interviewing and getting hired! You may often find yourself in circumstances where the people you are considering for employment have greater skills in their part of the hiring process than you.

Ineffective hiring skills result in many negative or detrimental outcomes. Among them are

- Selecting candidates who perform poorly
- Hiring candidates with disruptive behavior patterns
- Turning away some exceptional candidates
- Lowering overall productivity and quality of organizational performance
- An increase in hiring costs incurred by repeating the hiring process over and over
- The hindrance of future organizational growth
- The disruption of your managerial and leadership activities (Key question: What could you be doing if you weren't investing your time in rehiring?)

Exceptional hiring skills, including top-quality selection and retention abilities, not only enhance your career they also position the organization to meet and exceed its goals. Exceptional hiring skills are among the most desirable leadership skills in today's workplace. Managers at any level who demonstrate such sought-after skills are extremely visible and in great demand. A positive reality is that enhancing your skill to recognize talent, to bring it onboard, and to retain it for an extended time, makes you a very valuable organizational asset. The full spectrum of managerial excellence is considered to include the abilities to

- Identify exceptional candidates
- Successfully recruit candidates for the organization
- Accurately diagnose performance and process problems
- Identify and correct problems dealing with performance, disruptive behaviors, and process issues

- Develop the skills of the employees
- Retain peak performers for the long term

To a fault, many frontline managers restrict or impede their success by viewing the hiring process as a short-term effort merely intended to address current circumstances. In reality, the process is tactical as well as strategic both in the long term and in the short term. It offers an opportunity to upgrade the organization by selecting candidates who can meet the challenges of today and tomorrow. Hiring decisions are always an opportunity to upgrade the status quo.

The ability to recruit, interview, and select requires a specific set of skills, including the ability to predict future employee performance and behavior and to secure a meaningful commitment for dedicated efforts from a candidate. You should separate reality from illusion. You must have the skill to see through candidates' self-serving positive presentations of themselves and then determine the true levels of ability they possess. You must develop the talent to suppress your own enthusiasm and avoid falsely or inaccurately transferring to candidates the skills you want them to have. Left untrained and underdeveloped, you can be your own worst enemy in recruiting, interviewing, and selecting candidates.

This important process is not intended to determine:

- Whether you like them.
- Whether they give you a warm fuzzy feeling.
- Whether they are just like you in their abilities and skill sets.

The process does include your predicting whether candidates will provide significant future contributions to the organization and determining whether you and the organization are capable of meeting a candidate's needs over an extended period to ensure continued productivity.

In the past, the tasks of recruiting, interviewing, and selecting were primarily the domain of human resources professionals; today these responsibilities are passing to those in frontline management positions. More and more, managers who are ultimately responsible for performance are making final hiring decisions. If you are supported by a human resources department, it is probably doing the initial screening of candidates and then placing the hiring decision in your hands. Even if you do not make the final decision, you have probably seen a significant increase in your influence over the final selection. If you do not have the support of human resources professionals, you may be conducting the entire process yourself. Either way, you have increased responsibility. In today's workplace, frontline managers justifiably demand more involvement in the hiring process because of their increased accountability for their employees' behavior and performance. If you are going to be held accountable, you want to have your say in choosing the players on your team! It is difficult for managers and borders on unfairness when they are held responsible for the performance of people they haven't selected.

Organizations have also learned through negative experiences that not involving frontline managers in the hiring process creates an obvious path for deflecting responsibility and blame. Frontline managers frequently proclaim, "I can't be held responsible for the performance of someone else's candidates. I can't be accountable if I can't choose my people." Managers want to be successful and are willing to accept increased responsibility and accountability. They demand more control over the hiring selections that influence their fate.

Lack of involvement blurs the lines of accountability; involvement without training and skill development invites mediocrity or failure.

The Challenges

As a frontline manager, you experience many escalating challenges in the recruiting, interviewing, and selecting process of exceptional candidates. This complex task is far more difficult today than ever before in our economic history. The skills and behaviors that were effective in the past will not necessarily define success in today's workplace.

Among these challenges are

The Influence of Technology

The explosion of technology has permanently altered the recruiting, hiring, and retention process. Technology influences

- Who you want to hire
- The skills you want to hire
- How you hire the people you want
- The speed of information available to candidates
- The candidates' potential to pursue more career opportunities

Technology has had many positive influences on the hiring process, but it also creates significant impediments to you in your quest to hire exceptional candidates. The force of technology strengthens from minute to minute.

The Talent Drought

Fewer people are available to fill your staffing needs. Various factors influence this drought, including the health of the economy (when unemployment is low, fewer people are available, and so forth). When the economy fluctuates, availability fluctuates. In strong economic times, people have more job options available to them; this increases the pressure on managers and organizations to work hard in keeping productive employees satisfied.

The strong technology-driven economy has made a tremendous dent in how many qualified people are in the job market. The constant shifting of the economy creates a much higher demand for certain skill sets and decreases the value of others. Technology-based skills are now at a premium; the skills that fed our previously manufacturing-based economy are no longer as attractive or necessary. Service capabilities and high-quality interpersonal skills are also increasing in value. You are faced with the dual problems of fewer people in the job market and a scarcity of the skills needed to increase productivity and growth. These problems create an opportunity for you, as a frontline manager, to train and develop internally the skills you require. It may be necessary to hire candidates and train them rather than attempt to find the precise skill package you seek in those who are available. Today's frontline manager, regardless of title, is called upon more and more to be a teacher and a trainer.

The demographic makeup of available candidates is a major factor that is increasing in influence almost daily. You will face the repercussions of this challenge for many years to come. As the baby boomer generation leaves the workplace, fewer people are available to replace them. Severe shortages of skill-specific workers are increasing, and the situation is only going to get worse. According to Bill Styring, senior fellow at the Hudson Institute, in an interview with *Inc. Magazine*, "The current ratio of probable workers (ages 25–64) to probable retirees (ages 65 and over) is 4 to 1. By 2011, the first of the 76 million boomers will start to retire, driving the ratio to 3 to 1 in 2020, and it will approach 2 to 1 in 2030."*

This prediction indicates a serious implosion of the workforce that will affect organizations far into the twenty-first century.

The Visibility and Appeal of Specific Sectors of the Economy

High-tech dot com organizations have been very popular and have enjoyed the advantage of being able to attract high-caliber employment candidates. These companies have been able to skim the cream of the crop. As the future of some of these companies becomes uncertain, their appeal to high-quality candidates is changing. This is just another example of the effect of economic fluctuations.

Old-line, traditional, brick-and-mortar organizations increasingly find themselves less attractive to exceptional candidates and at a disadvantage in hiring and retention. The retail industry, once an attractive option for many, has lost its luster as potential candidates find appealing alternatives from which to choose. Certain strategies can increase your success when recruiting from a position of weakness, and later in this book we will explore the options. Although there are no magic formulas, and you certainly will not land every candidate whom you pursue, you need not accept less qualified or desirable candidates.

---

* Christopher Cagliano, "Recruiting Secrets," *Inc. Magazine* (October 1998): 32.

The Legal Issues of Hiring and Retention

Never before in our economic history have frontline managers been compelled to deal with the explosion of legal regulations. Among the laws that apply to hiring and employment are

- The Civil Rights Acts of 1964 and 1991
- The Pregnancy Discrimination Act of 1978
- The Vocational Rehabilitation Act of 1973
- The Vietnam Era of Veterans Readjustment Assistance Act of 1974
- The Polygraph Protection Act of 1988
- The Americans With Disabilities Act of 1990
- The Fair Labor Standards Act as amended by the Equal Pay Act

Although it is not within the scope of this book to address legal issues or to offer legal advice, it is critically important that you be aware of the legal implications in the hiring and employment process. Creating managerial awareness about legal issues is done to avoid liability, and most organizations do an adequate job. If this awareness training is not available to you, it is your responsibility to seek it from outside sources. Your legal representatives can offer valuable guidance; accurate and timely information is available through local universities and community colleges as well as from professional business and legal-training organizations. In later chapters, you will find general guidelines concerning legally sensitive interviewing issues and questions to be avoided.

Increased Collaboration Between Frontline Managers and Human Resources

In the past, the hiring process was controlled primarily or exclusively by the human resources department. If you had a job opening, you informed human resources and they recruited and hired a candidate for you. In many cases, only one individual would be offered for your final approval, and rejecting this chosen candidate was a difficult and sometimes career-damaging decision. Today, you are an increasingly important part of the hiring team, and you must take responsibility for sharpening your skills and responding to your increased opportunities. You must involve yourself in such ongoing recruiting activities as networking, development of referrals, and a constant outreach that previously was not typically considered a part of your responsibility. It is in your favor to seize all opportunities and exert as much influence as possible over the hiring and recruiting process to enhance your current and future success. Even if you can avoid participating in this process, it is not in your best interest to do so. Avoiding involvement because of a lack of time or because you place a low priority on recruiting and hiring is a cardinal managerial sin. Times have changed.

Increased Managerial Accountability and Liability

Your responsibility and accountability for the performance and behavior of your staff and, in some cases, for the consequences of their personal behavior, is increasing. You are expected to produce high returns from new employees at a greatly accelerated rate; and in today's workplace, employee weaknesses or disruptive behaviors show up in a considerably shorter time. Organizational and individual liability for the behaviors of employees has increased. Negligent hiring can be a legal basis for organizational as well as personal liability if it is proved that employers could or should have known that an employee was unfit for a position, or perhaps capable of criminal or tortuous behavior. If an employee is required to operate equipment, including automobiles, you can be held responsible if that employee causes damage and has a previous record of violations, such as driving while impaired or under the influence. You, as a manager, must exercise reasonable care when hiring to ensure that an employee's incompetence or unreliability does not cause risk of injury or damage to fellow employees, customers, or the public in general. You may also be considered responsible if someone you hired demonstrates personal behaviors that embarrass the organization or somehow result in bad publicity. The stakes involved in your hiring decisions are increasing daily.

Candidates View Employment Opportunities as Short Term

As everyone knows, people change jobs more frequently today than ever before. These job changes may be elected or involuntary. In many instances, employment is disrupted through reorganizing, downsizing, upsizing, restructuring—whatever the current popular term may be for head-count reduction. People are aware that, for the most part, guaranteed employment with an organization no longer exists. The bonds of loyalty have been broken in both directions. Organizational loyalty to employees and employees' loyalty to their employers has eroded. This is especially true among younger workers entering the workplace. They have seen their parents experience the pain and disruption of job loss through no fault of their own and realize that investing emotionally in a job and expecting long-term stability is unrealistic. Many business schools today encourage their students to plan for incremental job changes and suggest that four to five years is an optimum time to stay with one organization. In many industries, such as those most influenced by technology, that optimum time is reduced to twelve to eighteen months. Many new employees are planning their next career move the day they begin employment with you!

Because the candidates you consider are likely to be viewing your employment opportunity as a short-to-medium-term option, the benefits you offer must be tailored for immediate appeal. Your great retirement program, so important in the past, may no longer be so attractive. Career growth, skill enhancement, and accelerated incentives become more and more necessary from a recruiting perspective.

We will discuss hiring incentives and identifying many alternatives for you and your organization to consider in later chapters. While you may not have authority to influence the structuring of opportunities and incentives, you can begin to offer suggestions, and exert some influence over your organization's offerings.

Retaining Employees Is Becoming Critical

Your efforts to extend a peak performer's time of service become paramount. Perhaps you cannot keep employees until retirement; however, there is great benefit to you and the organization if you can extend their service from one year to three, or from four years to ten. Think of the improvement that would make in your overall productivity! Highly creative and productive people continue their employment if they believe their needs are being met as well as the needs of the organization. The effect of management skills on retention is monumental. It has been said that "people don't leave organizations, they leave managers." The bottom line: Good managers keep their people; bad managers run them off. If employees receive job offers elsewhere, the chances are that poor relationships with their managers had them looking in the first place! Excellent managerial effort plays a huge role in retention. You are an instrument of time of service extension.

A bad manager in a good organization experiences unacceptable turnover, lower rates of productivity, and increased incidents of disruptive employee behavior. An exceptional manager, even in a bad organization, experiences just the opposite. Management skills do matter in retaining employees and in extending their time of service. Although not all factors affecting retention are within your sphere of influence, we will identify in later chapters various opportunities for you to exert your positive managerial influence in keeping peak performers.

The Shift in the Balance of Power to Candidates

In the past, organizations took the attitude that "if employment candidates were lucky and they made a good enough impression, you would give them a break and extend a job offer." That attitude today will put you out of business! That type of hiring environment resides on the scrap heap of history, right along with the archaic medical practices of bleeding people or applying leeches to promote healing.

Today, candidates interview and evaluate organizations and managers just as much as they are being evaluated. Attractive candidates typically have multiple offers and they try to determine the option that best meets their interests and overall objectives. Highly creative and productive people no longer accept the next job offer; they evaluate the best job offer.

Just as you evaluate candidates by asking yourself, "Can this person help me and the organization achieve our overall goals?

Will this person make a positive contribution?" today's candidates evaluate you and ask, "Is this a manager I want to work for? Will this job enhance my career? Is this an organization that I want to be a part of?"

The hiring process is no longer a one-sided exercise favorably slanted toward the employer. You have to market yourself and your opportunity as highly desirable and more attractive than competitive offers. Many candidates shop for new managers just as much as they shop for new jobs!

The Shift of Workplace Motivation

The factors driving motivation and job satisfaction have shifted dramatically in today's workplace. In the past, people were motivated primarily by fear. The fear was rooted in the protection against the loss of economic stability; people did not want to lose the security they had worked hard to acquire. The overall attitude was, "I've got a pretty good job, I'm making okay money (never enough, but okay), and I have benefits, security, retirement, and I don't want to lose what I have worked hard to obtain." If their economic security was threatened directly or by implied message, employees were motivated to increase their performances or eliminate disruptive behaviors. The threat was effective. Today, employees are motivated not by fear but by gain. The overall attitude is, "What do I get from my job? Are my needs being met? Is my value being raised?" As long as employees believe their needs are being addressed and they are benefiting from the conditions of their employment, they tend to stay and be productive. When the gain or payoff is no longer evident, highly creative, highly productive people move on, a critical factor in the mobility of today's workforce. People are no longer willing to submit to fear-based management.

Although each individual defines gain differently, several common issues drive job satisfaction today; we will discuss these when we focus on the skills needed to keep peak performers.

Highly creative and productive people usually do not stay in an organizational environment if their perceptions of gain are not being met. Mediocre and poor performers do stay (along with people who believe, correctly or not, that they have no options). Even when they stay in a poor employment environment, employees usually rebel against it through lower productivity, through increased passive/aggressive resistant behaviors, and through negative attitudes that impede achievement and growth. The employees you really want to keep, move on; the people you don't necessarily want to keep, stay! That is not a formula for success!

Fierce Competition for Exceptional Candidates

If you are interested in a candidate, chances are great that other organizations are competing for that person's services. In light of this, you must be prepared to move fast in your recruiting and hiring efforts. The window of opportunity to employ an attractive candidate is short. When desirable candidates enter the job market, whether through job loss or through a decision to change jobs, they look for jobs only as long as they want to keep looking. If they want to be employed soon, they can make that happen; if they want to conduct extensive, in-depth searches, they have that option as well. Competing organizations, realizing that time is of the essence, are packaging attractive offers and urging candidates to make quick decisions and thereby limit lost opportunities. This tactic puts tremendous pressure on you and your organization to accelerate your process. Such acceleration does not mean that standards should be lowered or that necessary steps in the hiring process should be ignored; yet it does demand that wasted time be eliminated and your process must move at the speed of today's competitive business.

Recruiting Efforts Must Be Perpetual

In the past, recruiting efforts occurred only on an incremental or as-needed basis. If there was a need to fill a position, recruiting began and then was suspended until the next need arose. Today, your search for peak performers is a never-ending journey. It is an eternal quest. Even in the absence of immediate need, you must constantly anticipate the needs of tomorrow. The peak performer you hire next year may be the result of a recruiting seed you planted today. You never know when exceptional candidates will emerge and present opportunities for unexpected growth or organizational upgrade. In today's workplace, the perception that you are not hiring can put you on the fast track to oblivion! Even if you have no immediate need, you and your organization may be willing to create opportunity if an optimum candidate suddenly appears. That appearance will take place only if you are constantly vigilant in your recruiting efforts. You are always recruiting.

Hiring Traps

A lack of training in the hiring process, the pace of today's business, and the increase in responsibilities often lead front-line managers into hiring traps. When recruiting and interviewing are added to your other tasks; when intense short-term emphasis is placed on productivity; when immediate goals must be met; and when daily crises and problems must be solved, there is little wonder that the hiring process may suffer. It is not because you lack willingness. It is because you lack available time to meet all your objectives and responsibilities.

Hiring managers typically fall prey to ten traps, and throughout this book you will learn skills and strategies to avoid or overcome them. The first step in any preventative effort is awareness. To avoid falling into these traps, you must know where they lie.

Trap #1—Lack of Preparation

The most pervasive and problematic of all the traps is lack of preparation. Its impact contributes to the creation of other traps and negative outcomes.

Failure to prepare properly results in

- Unclear hiring objectives
- Entering the hiring process without understanding the specific skills you want to hire
- Ineffective, off-the-cuff interviews that result in frontline managers relying on instinct or making gut-hunch hiring decisions

Candidate selections made as a result of poor preparation are typically driven by subjective feelings, not objective criteria.

Effective preparation will be discussed extensively in subsequent chapters.

Trap #2—Talking Too Much

Because of improper planning, lack of training, and low confidence in the process, many frontline managers try to "wing it" and end up dominating the hiring and interviewing process by talking too much. They just sit down, start talking, and hope for the best! Some frontline managers begin interviews by saying, "Let me tell you about us" or "Let me tell you all about me." They talk incessantly throughout the interviews while the candidates listen attentively, smile appropriately, and "ooh" and "aah" at the right times. When the interview sessions are over, these managers instinctively feel good about the candidate! Why? Because the candidates allowed the managers to talk about their favorite subjects—themselves and their organizations. Of course, these managers like the candidates. We all like people who listen to us! The candidates do an excellent job of impressing the managers, however, little or nothing has been learned about the candidates' backgrounds and qualifications or their potential for performance. The hiring decision is based on a gut hunch with little or no specific information to support the conclusion.

Your ability to ask effective questions and listen to and carefully evaluate candidates' responses are the foundation for effective hiring. Frontline managers hire effectively by listening, not by always talking. Will Rogers once said, "Never miss a good chance to shut up." His comment is valuable advice when you are interviewing.

Trap #3—Egg-Timer Decisions

The propensity of some managers to rely on instinct and gut hunch results in their making quick subjective decisions. Sometimes a manager subconsciously decides within the first three to five minutes of an interview either to include a candidate in the pool of potential hires or to exclude the candidate from consideration. In about the same time it takes to cook a soft-boiled egg, the manager makes an impulsive decision and spends the rest of the interview seeking information to support that decision. Please understand, this rush to judgment is rarely intentional or even a conscious effort. It flourishes when managers lack training, plan poorly, and base their hiring decisions on instinct. A frontline manager may soon determine that he is not interested in a candidate and then begin asking negative questions to which a candidate cannot possibly offer a positive response. Conversely, a manager may quickly realize that she does have an interest in a candidate and begin asking "softball" questions that allow the candidate to present himself in a positive light.

Even managers who are highly skilled at hiring must be aware of this tendency to make unrealistic, unfair, inefficient, unreasonable, and quick decisions.

Trap #4—Periscope-Depth Questioning

This is the tendency to ask inch-deep and mile-wide interview questions without delving extensively into relevant issues or pursuing the red flags that may surface. Effective interviewing and hiring demands mile-deep and inch-wide probing, and the gathering of as much information as possible about relevant issues and specific skills. Many frontline managers either do not recognize or intentionally avoid pursuing areas of importance or concern. (Again, usually the result of a lack of training or poor planning.) In Chapter 2, we will discuss the importance of developing realistic needs assessments and of determining exactly what you want to know about a candidate. If you really don't know what you are looking for, it is difficult to ask the right questions. Shallow or periscope-depth questioning leaves you in the dark!

Trap #5—Poor Understanding of Needs and Inefficient Communication of True Wants

Lack of preparation also makes it difficult to communicate to anyone else involved in the hiring process your true hiring needs and the specific skill sets you are looking for in candidates. This is especially critical when the human resources department is involved in the initial screening of candidates. Although their support is valuable in the preliminary screening, interviewing, and culling of candidates, they must understand what you are looking for. If you do not effectively communicate the parameters of the search or your definition of exceptional and unacceptable candidates, they will probably select people who do not meet your needs. You may end up settling for marginal candidates. In the absence of your clear communication, others involved will understandably insert their own perceptions into the selection process. They may even revert to using preexisting or obsolete job descriptions as the basis for the selection criteria, resulting in less than desirable candidates from which to choose. If this happens, it probably won't be the fault of others!

Unquestionably, the primary responsibility falls to you for evaluating and effectively communicating the selection criteria. The process is too important to leave to chance or to the unguided perceptions of others.

Trap #6—Rating Individual Strengths Disproportionately

This is the potential pitfall of focusing on one or two factors of a candidate's strengths and overlooking other negatives or significant weaknesses. As an example, if you are looking for a candidate with a specific technical skill, you may be so happy to find someone who possesses that ability that you fail to realize that his weaknesses in some other important areas could doom him to failure. Evaluate all factors proportionately. Do not allow skill strengths to overshadow significant weaknesses. Jack the Ripper possessed excellent "cutting" skills, but he also showed substantial behavioral weaknesses that would have made him a problem employee! Managers too often fall prey to seeing in a candidate exactly what they want to see.

Trap #7—Hiring Your Own Image

It is also a common tendency for managers to hire people who are most like themselves. In its most vile form, this is the basis for discriminatory hiring practices in which employment is denied to certain people because they are different. For most of you, this trap does not result in blatantly discriminatory hiring practices. It is usually an unconscious and unintended attempt to surround yourself with people you are most comfortable with, which generally means people who are most like you. Liking people who are similar to us is a human trait. Although that can be a strength when planning a party, it is a weakness when hiring employees! Hiring in your own image ignores issues of diversity. Organizational diversity is frequently the bedrock of organizational strength. Similar-image hiring usually means that existing strengths tend to be reinforced (which may not be necessary) and existing weaknesses tend to be exacerbated (which may be deadly). The truth is, you probably don't need people who are strong in the same areas of personal strength that you possess. You will benefit from hiring people who can offset your personal and your organizational weaknesses. This means hiring people who may be different, or who bring different skill sets to your workplace. Some weak or inefficient managers fear others who possess skills superior or different from their own. They may even discourage or turn down candidates they see as posing a performance threat. Talk about insecurity! In today's workplace such dysfunctional behavior results in additional job opportunities for managerial positions because these managers soon find themselves unemployed!

Hiring in your own image is, at worst, illegal and immoral; at best, it is inefficient.

Trap #8—Fog-the-Mirror Hiring

Frequently referred to as panic hiring, it is merely hiring "warm bodies," that is, hiring all who are available regardless of experience or abilities. It is the equivalent of placing a mirror under the nostrils of potential candidates, and if they fog the mirror and can prove they really do have stable vital signs, you offer them a job! This practice places a greater emphasis on filling a job rather than on the quality and abilities of those you choose to serve the organization. Interestingly, this trap can occur with organizations that are experiencing explosive growth. When things are growing at a frantic pace, some managers believe they have little or no time to dedicate to the hiring process. Few strategies slow growth and feed disaster faster or more devastatingly than hiring warm bodies. This trap also occurs when the responsibility for hiring is delegated to others who see it as a low priority. Someone else may be willing to hire a warm body for you. Don't allow that to happen. Fog-the-mirror candidates do not perform adequately and they force you to revisit the hiring process repeatedly and at great cost to you and the organization. Unfortunately, fog-the-mirror candidates frequently become permanent employees who continue to drain organizational resources. The reactionary short-term strategy of hiring anyone who walks through the door always yields disastrous long-term consequences.

Trap #9—Hiring the Best Available Versus a Patient Search

Different from egg-timer, or fog-the-mirror hiring, this trap addresses the willingness to accept expediently the best available candidate even though he or she may not meet your overall expectations or possess the skill sets you have established as necessary for success. This is settling on the best candidate available at that moment rather than continuing to search for a legitimate peak performer. This trap is usually influenced by perceived time pressures. Understandably, you are tempted to hire the best available when production issues are at stake or you have other pressing issues that demand your time. Hiring the best available is a short-term strategy that can have definite, negative, long-term implications. An exceptional candidate might have been available had you only been willing to continue your search for even a short time, but you will never know if you fall into trap #9. Lengthening or expanding a search may yield candidates with far greater potential. The pool of current available candidates is just a snapshot of one point in time. Hiring the best available may preclude you from hiring the best ever!

Trap #10—Creating a Negative First Impression

Just as the first impression a candidate gives you is extremely important in your perception of that candidate, you must also be aware of the importance of the first impression you and the organization project to a candidate. As we discussed earlier, candidates are interviewing you and your organization as well as submitting to your review of them. What impression do candidates form within the first three minutes of the interview? Do you spend the initial moments of an interview silently reviewing candidates' applications or resumes? (This should have been done before the interview.) Do candidates see your desk and filing system in a state of disorganization or disarray? Do you ignore candidates while you complete a phone call? (You are better off asking them to wait outside your office rather than ignoring them by being on the telephone.)

Real-World Example:

Larry was a manager in the internal auditing department of a major financial organization. The human resources recruiting specialist found what she described as an "excellent candidate who was highly motivated to join our company." When Larry began to interview the candidate, he interrupted the meeting to take an urgent phone call. Larry reacted badly to the information he received and launched into a "shoot the messenger" style of attack on the person on the phone. He raised his voice, used some inappropriate language, and ended the phone conversation by saying, "If this ever happens again, heads will roll." When Larry returned his attention to the candidate, she was unresponsive to his questioning and demonstrated little or no interest in the position. At the conclusion of the interview, being unimpressed, Larry fired off an e-mail to the recruiting specialist criticizing her ability to assess "excellent candidates."

Carefully consider the candidates' line of sight. What impressions will they form of you and the organization by what they see and hear during their initial interactions? The first impression candidates form of you and of your organization can have tremendous influence over their willingness to commit to employment and to remain employed long term.

Hiring Skills Assessment

On a scale of 1 to 5, rate your susceptibility to the ten hiring traps. (A rating of 1 indicates little or no susceptibility; in other words, you never fall into the traps. A rating of 5 indicates the traps represent significant hiring challenges for you.) Be wary of the natural tendency to rate yourself inappropriately high

Lack of preparation	1 2 3 4 5
Talking too much	1 2 3 4 5
Egg-timer decisions	1 2 3 4 5
Periscope-depth questioning	1 2 3 4 5
Lack of clear understanding of need and communication of true wants	1 2 3 4 5
Disproportionately rating individual strengths	1 2 3 4 5
Hiring in your own image	1 2 3 4 5
Fog-the-mirror hiring	1 2 3 4 5
Hiring the best available vs. a patient search	1 2 3 4 5
Creating a negative first impression	1 2 3 4 5

A rating of 3 or above indicates an opportunity for improvement and should serve as the basis for your overall action plan in processing the rest of the information in this book. We will present skills and options to help you avoid all the traps. Decide which techniques are relevant to you; then assess the level of your commitment to improve your recruiting and hiring skills.

In Chapter 2, we will discuss the importance of planning and developing real-world needs assessments.

2

Developing Real-World Needs Assessments

There are four phases in your quest to find, hire, and keep peak-performing employees.

First is the *planning* phase:

- Determining the exact skills, experience, behaviors you want to hire
- Identifying where you can find the people you want to attract to your organization
- Discovering what will make these attractive candidates respond positively to you and your organization
- Preparing to interview effectively to ensure the success of your hiring efforts

Second is the *buying* phase:

- Determining whether you have an interest in specific candidates and want to pursue them for potential employment

- Predicting the levels of contribution they can make to the organization
- Discovering their true skills

Phase three is the *selling* phase:

- Presenting yourself, your organization, and your career opportunity in an honest and favorable light
- Generating interest and excitement in the high quality candidates you pursue
- Having candidates commit and follow through when joining your organization

The final phase is *skill development and retention:*

- Ensuring the candidates you hire perform to their greatest ability for an extended period

The greater your ability to develop your employees, the more willing they are to learn; and the longer you can keep them employed, the more productivity they will contribute.

The Importance of a Needs Assessment

This chapter is focused on the first aspect of the planning phase. We will address the critical importance of determining the skill sets that are necessary for success in the candidates you pursue. Many managers do not take the time to define what they are searching for. In Chapter 1, we identified lack of preparation as the primary hiring trap and the root cause of many other hiring problems. The first stage of preparation is developing a real-world needs assessment. Failing to do so is the equivalent of going to the grocery store when you are hungry and without a prepared shopping list. The typical result will be not buying the things you really need; impulsively selecting unnecessary items; spending more money than you intended to; having to return to the store to gather all the things you should have acquired in the first place.

Developing an effective needs assessment allows you to prepare your shopping list to avoid problems!

There is not one generic set of overall skill competencies. One size does *not* fit all. You are not always looking for the same things. Every job has different requirements, and those requirements undergo constant change. The skills that are necessary for success today are far different from those that were necessary for the same job three to five years ago! The skills required for tomorrow's success will be far different from today's. If you do not take the time to evaluate your current hiring situation properly and plan your recruiting effort, the hiring process will be built upon a crumbling foundation.

Many managers attempt to fly by the seat of their pants and bring an "I'll know it when I see it" attitude to recruiting and hiring. They con themselves into thinking that they possess a magic ability to size up candidates quickly, and they pride themselves on making hiring decisions solely on instinct and gut hunch. Managers who do this should quit their jobs and start their own "psychic hotline." In reality, all they are doing is making an egg-timer decision on whether they *like* a candidate and fall far short of identifying a candidate's true strengths and weaknesses.

Developing a comprehensive real-world needs assessment is also of critical importance when others are involved in the hiring process. If human resources or anyone else is going to attract, screen initial candidates, or support your efforts in any way, they have to know what you are looking for if their support is going to be effective. If inconsistencies linger in the perceptions of the required skill sets necessary for success, your needs and the candidates others select will likely not match up.

John Korzec is the Director of Human Resources for the Otis Elevator Company's plant in Bloomington, Indiana. Otis Elevator Company is a 150-year-old elevator manufacturing, installation, and service company. John had this comment concerning the importance of needs assessments:

> I think because they are so busy, it is sometimes difficult to get frontline managers to take the necessary time to describe exactly what they are looking for in a candidate. And although this sounds painfully easy, I think it's much more difficult than it sounds. I think it's important to probe and challenge people to define the characteristics they are really looking for and how those characteristics will lead to the accomplishment and attainment of the goals they want the organization and this particular person to achieve. A manager may indicate he wants a change agent candidate, but it is important to probe to determine whether it is someone to introduce radical change or a more programmed evolutionary type of low-pain change. It is very important for frontline managers to sit down and think through their needs.

John acknowledged that the development of a preplanned needs assessment does not always occur and that miscommunications and disconnects frequently happen:

> A lot of times this disconnect does not flush itself out until after you've interviewed one or two candidates. It's good news when everyone involved can get on the same page. It's bad news if you fail to do so and end up making strategically bad hiring decisions. Every time you hire someone it represents an opportunity

to improve and upgrade the organization. Every hiring decision needs to be treated as strategic as well as tactical for the organization. Some managers have a tendency to want to preserve the status quo when making hiring decisions. It's important to pressure, probe, and challenge the current thinking to make sure you're taking advantage of the opportunity, not to simply maintain the status quo, but to enhance the capability of the organization by upgrading the talent pool.

Criteria for Needs Assessment

Creating an effective needs assessment begins with asking yourself these key questions:

- What do I want to accomplish by filling this position?
- Which skills made others successful in the past?
- Which skill weaknesses contributed to past failures?
- How has this job changed?
- Which additional skills will be necessary to achieve success in the future?

Once these questions have been considered, you can begin to compile your hiring criteria. An effective assessment encompasses a minimum of five action points.

1. Evaluate the Existing Written Job Description

If a written job description exists, it is a good place to *start*. However, keep in mind it is a valuable *piece* of the puzzle. It is not the only determining factor upon which to base the entire needs assessment. In reality, most job descriptions become obsolete as soon as the ink dries on the paper. Responsibilities and challenges change so rapidly that job descriptions quickly become painfully out-of-date. The way the job was structured when the formal job description was completed may be far different from its current reality. It has often been said that the devil is in the details, and as far as job descriptions are concerned, the devil is usually in the phrase "other duties as assigned." Those duties often become dominant components of the job responsibilities. Emerging tasks may increase in importance and dwarf tasks that may have once been seen as areas of primary responsibility. Are the skills required to accomplish the accumulated "other duties as assigned" different from those in the formal job description?

In many organizations, job descriptions are used exclusively as the total basis for determining a needs assessment. Candidates are sought who meet the obsolete, inconsistent, or perhaps irrelevant criteria, and the actual needs of today and tomorrow remain unconsidered. Consider the formal job description and look past its restrictive boundaries to identify additional needs as the first step in creating a meaningful shopping list.

2. Seek the Input of Individuals Who Do the Job

Identify and evaluate your current peak performers. Seek their input on what they believe to be the most important factors that allow them to accomplish their current levels of success. What you or other managers perceive to be the most important skills contributing to success may be different to the perceptions of those who are doing the job.

Real-World Example:

Laura was an assistant marketing manager for a fast-paced software development company. In her organization, the assistant marketing manager's job was an important stress-filled position. It offered a fast track to promotion, demotion, or termination! The AMMs were continuously assigned projects to complete under the direction of the senior marketing managers. If they developed a consistent record of success, they were eligible for lucrative bonuses and significant promotional opportunities. It was a position in which employees quickly succeeded or failed, and only one in six AMMs lasted more than nine months with the organization. AMM was considered a make-it-or-break-it, burnout position. Typically, the company sought candidates who were recent college graduates with marketing degrees and strong written communication skills.

Laura was extremely successful, and after twenty-four months as an AMM, she was promoted to a regional sales manager's position. In preparing to seek Laura's replacement, her current manager asked her three questions:

- What was the key to your success as an assistant marketing manager?
- What skills do you possess that allowed you to succeed where many others have failed?
- What additional skills should we be looking for in hiring your replacement?

Laura's answers were specific, with one primary theme: the importance of organizational skills. She said, "So much emphasis has been placed on marketing and communication skills, and although those are extremely important, people are going to survive in this pressure cooker only if they are organized. I've seen others fail because they couldn't keep all the balls in the air. We seem to take great pains to hire people with specific backgrounds, yet we don't look at their organizational skills. We don't evaluate them, nor do we teach them. I guess we just expect people to be automatically organized. We have had a number of people who were just as good as I am, if not better, in their marketing skills, yet they failed. The difference was that I had better overall organizational skills. This job will bury you in e-mails, crises, and urgent requests, and if you can't organize them, you will go down in a blaze of failure. I am amazed we don't put organizational skills on the top of our list."

Laura brought a valuable insight and a more complete understanding of the skills necessary to succeed in the job she was vacating. Her manager began to seek candidates with exceptional organizational skills and instituted a preemployment competency test to assess those skills accurately. The manager also requested that the training department present a series of training programs to enhance the organizational skills of all employees. Her information provided the opportunity to re-create the needs assessment by blending the formal job description with first-hand experience.

After talking with Laura, her manager was also seen walking around, smacking his forehead with his open palm, and mumbling, "Duh . . . why didn't I think of that?"

It is amazing what you can learn if you will only take the time to ask and to listen.

3. Discussions with Customers

Carefully identify the external and internal customers the potential candidate will be asked to serve. Customers are a valuable source of insight into identifying the skills necessary for success. Ask them three questions:

- Which skills possessed by people in this job serve you well?

- Which skills lacked by people in this job are a hindrance to you?
- Which skills do you think we should stress in our hiring search?

Their responses will give you additional information, including emphasis of the skills you should continue to seek; additional skills for your consideration; and awareness that some skills may no longer be as important.

External and internal customers may offer you the best information for creating a meaningful needs assessment. Customers may have a different perception of the criteria for success than you.

Real-World Example:

A large public school district was hiring four additional technicians for its information technology department. These new employees would be responsible for installing new computer equipment in the district's high schools, training the teachers and administrative staff to use the new resources properly, and responding to ongoing technical or service problems. These technicians would work closely with the schools' principals. When the principals were asked for their input concerning the hiring criteria for the new employees, one message was received loud and clear: They wanted technicians who have the ability to communicate highly complex information to all the teachers and the administrative support staff who were nontechnical personnel. They did not want people who could communicate only with other "techies." One principal said, "Training the computer science teacher on this new technology is going to be far different from training the history teacher and the football coach. We need technicians who can communicate effectively with everyone, regardless of an employee's technical knowledge.

We are tired of being either talked down to or confused by a lot of technical jargon."

This input helped the frontline hiring decisionmaker in the I.T. department realize that technical skills were not enough in the candidates she hired. In the past, technical skills were the primary hiring criteria. She now realized she needed technicians with strong communication and teaching skills as well.

4. Your Personal Observations, Assessments, and Predictions

In line with John Korzec's comments, it is important that you not only consider the immediate skill needs of today but attempt to determine the needs of tomorrow. Some significant questions to ask yourself:

- What do I think the next candidate in this position should be able to do differently?
- Is this an opportunity to restructure the job's requirements? If so, which current skills will be necessary?
- What new skills will be required for the expanded position?
- What additional skills would upgrade the department, group, team, or overall organization?

Considering these issues allows you to make strategic as well as tactical hiring decisions and gives you the opportunity to consider restructuring your department. You can put the resources of the staff in place to meet the emerging demands of change.

It is also important for you to consider the organization's vision and future goals, and to use that information as a basis for assessing your current and future needs.

5. Meeting the Specific Skills Needed Today While Assessing Your Ability and Willingness to Teach and Coach

There is no such thing as a perfect candidate. You must determine which specific skills a candidate must possess before you can consider him or her for employment and what skills you are willing and able to teach. It is essential that you evaluate the immediate critical skill needs as opposed to the potential development of the candidate. What are the nonnegotiable must-haves compared to the possibilities for growth? This evaluation should include not only the candidate's potential to grow and develop but also your realistic ability to teach and coach.

- Can you help the employee develop additional skills through your coaching efforts?
- Do you realistically have the time to dedicate to this development? (Lighting candles and saying prayers won't get it done.)
- Do you have the luxury of enough time to wait for the candidate to develop? (Never hire "potential" unless you have the "potential" to develop it!)

You must also consider the capabilities of your training department and whether you have the benefit of their support. (Not all organizations have a training department; many frontline managers are on their own.)

What additional training can they offer to assist in skill development? Do not fall prey to what *could* happen. Make decisions based on what *will* happen.

Needs Assessment Tool

The following is an example of a needs assessment tool you may find helpful.

What are the core responsibilities of the job? (List as many as necessary.)

_____ _____

_____ _____

_____ _____

What skills are essential to success for each core responsibility?	Urgency: Is this a skill a candidate must already possess to be considered for employment?	Can I/we train this skill short term?	Can I/we coach this skill long term?

Real-World Example:

Stephanie is a senior project manager and team leader for an environmental testing lab. She was managing three project managers and was given approval to add a fourth. She identified the core responsibilities for the new project manager's job as

- Client service and contact
- Prioritizing sample flow through the laboratory
- Distribution of sampling kits
- Auditing and reviewing regulatory permit requirements
- Project and price quoting

She then developed the following assessment:

What skills are essential to success for each core responsibility?	Urgency: Is this a skill a candidate must already possess to be considered for employment?	Can I/we train this skill short term?	Can I/we coach this skill long term?
Degreed in science	Yes	No	No
State licensing and certification	Yes	No	No
Strong organizational skills	Yes	No	No
Strong communication skills	Yes	No	No
Knowledge of chemical testing procedures	Yes	No	No
Mastery of the testing procedures	No	Yes	Yes
Knowledge of the computer system and software	No	Yes	Yes
Testing policies and lab procedures	No	Yes	Yes
Account knowledge	No	No	Yes
Project and price quote knowledge	No	No	Yes

This assessment allowed Stephanie to identify the skills every candidate must possess to be considered for the project manager's position. She was also able to evaluate and plan future training activities once the candidate was hired. She also determined that some of the training, including testing procedures, knowledge of the computer system and software, along with account knowledge, could be delegated to the existing team of project managers.

Using this tool and conducting an effective needs assessment will help you avoid these traps:

- Egg-timer decisions
- Failure to understand need and to communicate true wants
- Disproportionately rating individual strengths
- Hiring the best available instead of conducting a patient search

John Korzec added these additional thoughts concerning the importance of a needs assessment:

Another mistake I see made a lot is when multiple candidates go through the interviewing process and the decision is made to select one. In reality, this candidate may not satisfy all of the overall strategic needs of the organization. He may not represent an upgrade to the status quo. He might not fulfill some strategic hiring objectives you may have, like developing succession candidates for other positions. You just can't settle for the best available. You need to discipline yourself to identify what you are looking for, and don't settle for less. Assess what the critical characteristics are in the candidates and whether they have what it takes to be successful and meet *all* the needs of the organization. You should not make the hiring decision until you have checked all those blocks. As an example, we hire industrial engineers. It is pretty easy to round up a collection of four or five industrial engineers to interview and choose the best available. You may find an individual who has the right educational background, and who has the right experience in doing things such as time studies, routings and shop floor layouts. However, this same group of candidates may be lacking in critical leadership skills necessary to fill a longer-term need of having a pool of talent that is capable of filling supervisory or management positions in the near future. The organization may want someone who in three years can be ready to be the manager of industrial engineering and has the potential to lead people. You could hire a very decent industrial engineer yet fail to provide for the long-term needs of the organization. There is also the temptation to identify a critical strength of a candidate and accept that as being a strength for all of the critical characteristics of the job. Some managers perceive that being strong in one area equals being strong in all the other required areas. Past work experience is often an example. Managers may focus on a candidate's ten years' experience as an industrial engineer, which on the surface appears strong, yet perhaps fails to recognize some of the other critical aspects of the job. Soft skills, such as teamwork, interpersonal skills, and the ability to communicate effectively, are also very important. It is necessary to recognize the totally well-rounded picture.

The time to create the well-rounded picture is *before* the recruiting and hiring process begins.

Critical Areas of Evaluation

In developing a real-world needs assessment, you should consider at least seven areas of specific skills and qualifications.

The depth of these skills and qualifications and the weight of their importance will change according to the job. You must decide the situational priority placed on each one. The value you placed on specific skills in the past may not be the same for the hiring you do for today and tomorrow. The key to maximizing the effect of your evaluation is to identify *specific* skills. Avoid such global statements as

"She must have strong people skills."
"He must be a self-starter."
"She must have strong technical skills."
"He must be goal-oriented."

The problem with these high-sounding, all-encompassing statements is that no one knows what they really mean. The skills and qualifications you are looking for must be rooted in *specific* definitions and supported by specific behaviors.

Education (Including Licenses and Certifications)

What levels of education and what credentials must the successful candidate possess? It is important to reevaluate consistently your requirements for job relevancy. Do they really matter? If the answer is yes, then they become a nonnegotiable part of your needs assessment. Is it important that the candidate have a specific degree? Would you consider someone who is actively pursuing that degree or related credentials? (Not someone who is *telling* you he will pursue it, but someone who can document current enrollment in the course of study; there is a huge difference!) Many good candidates are overlooked because they may not meet your exact requirements. It can be either a waste of good talent if those requirements are not relevant or a critical indicator of high qualification if they are necessary. If you do not reevaluate and establish relevant requirements, you may be lowering your standards inadvertently. You may be looking for lesser-qualified candidates when you should be stressing higher levels of education or certification. This sword cuts both ways.

In many industries today, experience and demonstrated skill levels are being weighted more heavily than education requirements.

Experience

What levels of experience must the candidates possess? Must candidates have past experience in a specific industry? If so, how many years? Is it really relevant? Which carries more weight, educational background or years of experience? Are both equally important? Does one outweigh the other? Must your candidates have both?

When you evaluate experience, you must be aware that you are considering years of positive, valuable experience along with the same years of habitual weakness and bad habit. Just because candidates have done something similar somewhere else does not mean they will meet your objectives for organizational performance. Hiring experienced mediocrity perpetuates current and future mediocrity. You may be able to relax your requirements for experience if you possess effective skills in coaching or if the organization is capable of training and highly committed to it. Even with the most experienced candidates, training is necessary. No matter how experienced they are, you and your organization do things differently. All new employees must be trained in different policies, procedures, and techniques, with no exceptions made for experience. Also, experienced candidates usually require a considerable amount of "un-training." Previously learned bad habits or irrelevant skills will have to be erased before the new career opportunity can be completely accepted.

Another often-overlooked aspect of hiring experienced people concerns the existence of transferable skills. Is it necessary for a candidate to have done the same thing for an organization within your industry? Jobs that appear different may have many commonalties of skill. Expanding your vision and realizing that many skills are transferable can be rewarding. People who appear to have unrelated backgrounds may already be demonstrating the skills you are seeking, but in a different form. You will often find that position or function experience is more valuable than industry or task-specific experience. For example, someone highly skilled in customer service in one industry may be capable of transferring her skills to provide exceptional customer service in another industry. Industry knowledge may be easier to teach than the interactive skills necessary for serving customers well. Many people electing to make career changes are overlooked because they lack industry-specific experience. Highly capable and polished professionals are leaving the education and health-care industries because monumental changes are taking place in those environments. These people bring with them refined communication, conflict resolution, and, in some cases, technically oriented skills that can be readily transferred to other industries. However, if managers focus solely on specific industry or task experience, they might ignore excellent candidates.

If you are willing to consider candidates with transferable skills, you will broaden the recruiting pool.

Technical Skills

For many years it was said, "Hire people skills and train technical skills." This probably still has some current validity because the skills of interaction are often more difficult to teach and learn. In today's workplace, however, the dominant influence of technology demands that the candidates you hire have multiple skill sets.

There are two levels of technical skills.

The first level includes generalized technical skills. These deal with the technological demands of every job in today's economy. Most job classifications or functions require at least minimal computer skills. Even nontechnical positions require candidates to possess the technical proficiency to do the job and to adapt new technological skills as they become necessary.

Second are the specific technical skills and abilities required to meet the demands of the individual job. These may include testing procedures, operating equipment, calculating setups and tolerances, designing systems, and so on. They are the basic fundamental skills required to do the job. Such skills are often learned through education and experience; the manager can usually evaluate them before the final hiring decision.

Of all the areas of assessment, technical skills, education, and experience are the *easiest* to verify. Technical skills can be tested; education and experience can be readily confirmed. In common practice, most frontline managers limit their hiring assessments to these three primary areas because they lend themselves to black-and-white, clear-cut decisions. Unfortunately, they can lead to an incomplete hiring practice because four other critical areas should also be considered. These tend to be more difficult (but not impossible) to identify, and they are usually critical to the overall success of peak performers. The next four areas of evaluation often make the difference between mediocrity and excellence. Education, experience, and technical skills make candidates good; the skills they possess in motivation, organization, interaction, and collaboration make them great.

Motivation

Strong consideration must be given to the motivational factors concerning all candidates. Although every manager wants to hire people who come to work every day, do their jobs, are driven to exceed standards and objectives, and demand little or no managerial attention, such perfect, water-walking candidates are hard to find! You must also attempt to evaluate the alignment between the candidates' motivational needs, your managerial style, and the overall environment of the organization.

- Do you and the organization provide high levels of positive recognition?
- Do you offer "payoffs" for individual and group achievements?
- Do you use emotional appeals to increase performance?

If so, you should hire candidates who will respond to those external motivational strategies.

- Is the work motivating?
- Are your employees able to see the rewarding and positive outcomes of their work?
- Do they have the opportunity to witness healing, learning, growth development, and the enhancement of health, safety, and/or welfare in those they serve?

If so, the work may be so intrinsically rewarding that you do not have to provide external motivational stimulus—people will tend to do their jobs well just for the experience and opportunity of doing it.

Are you looking for candidates who are internally driven to seek perfection and consistently put forth their best effort regardless of the circumstances? Although such candidates are usually considered ideal, you must carefully assess the practicality of supporting such motivation. It is not quite as simple as it may appear. If employees are driven to perfection and peak performance, will you allow them to be perfect? Are you able to give them the time and resources they need in their pursuit of perfection? If you try to manage these employees too closely, you will drive them away. Are time and dollars your organizational environment's dominant consideration? If so, many internally motivated candidates will be frustrated by such limitations and perceive them as a hindrance to their achievement of exceptional quality. Quality has many definitions. Internally driven candidates may see your levels of quality acceptance as less than their own internal levels of acceptability. It is possible that top-quality candidates are seeking new opportunities and are available for your recruitment because they believe they are unsupported and unfulfilled in their current positions. Can you offer them a different environment, more conducive to their job satisfaction and performance? If not, they probably won't stay long even if you do hire them.

Other motivational factors to consider are the issues of

Adaptability   Willingness to take initiative
Flexibility   Integrity
Ability to embrace change

(Keep in mind, candidates may also be seeking new employment because they are uncomfortable with the changes in their current organizations. If they do not accept changes where they are, what makes you think they can deal with changes in your organization?)

An accurate assessment of motivational factors is a challenge; it must be considered carefully when you evaluate candidates. If you hire someone who is highly qualified but unmotivated, you will have performance problems. If you hire someone who is highly motivated but mediocre, you will have highly motivated mediocrity! Consider all factors in balance.

Organizational Skills

Frequently overlooked, such skills represent the ability to work in an organized fashion. This area includes

- Structuring tasks in a sequence so they can be accomplished efficiently
- Planning for the short term and the long term
- Maintaining a clean work area
- Setting priorities and measuring work
- Setting realistic goals

The importance of organizational skills is compounded because too many managers and organizations do a poor job of teaching them. The level of organizational skill employees bring with them will probably stay the same throughout their employment. Poor organizational skills are usually an unrecognized contributor to an employee's poor performance or failure. People who are disorganized tend to perceive themselves as highly stressed and are unable to take on additional assignments effectively. In today's environment of "doing more with less," you cannot do more if you do not possess the required organizational skills.

If you hire a disorganized candidate who is highly motivated, you end up with a *blizzard of disorganization!*

Interactive Skills

These are often considered the soft skills, or the people skills. They include

Effective communication	Customer service
Active listening	Conflict resolution
Decisionmaking	Risk taking
Problem solving	Establishing effective
	workplace relationships
Stress management	

In many circumstances, these are the most critical skills necessary to do an effective job. Poor interactive skills are often the weaknesses that cost people their jobs. Think about the people you have worked with who have been relieved of their duties; probably 80 percent of the time, their failures were rooted in poor interactive skills. Even employees in technical positions are being called upon to demonstrate effective interactive skills. For many managers and organizations, these are the most difficult skills to train. Because of this, it is critical that you identify the need and successfully evaluate a candidate's skill level. If you don't have success in training these skills, you had better hire them in the first place. The truth is, they *can* be trained; the candidates who possess these skills *learned* them somewhere!

Chemistry, Teamwork, and Collaboration

Often, the wild card in hiring is the key consideration of how candidates will fit in. This is *not* determining whether you or the people in the department will like the candidates; it is determining whether the candidates will make an effective contribution to the group. Will they bring unique strengths and help overcome existing weaknesses? Will they perform and behave in a manner that promotes group, team, and/or departmental harmony? The issue of *like* becomes neutralized. The key consideration is whether candidates will complement the existing environment and find that the existing circumstances meet their needs. This includes

- The ability to work in collaborative environments
- The willingness to allow others input and influence concerning their activities
- The wisdom to avoid turf battles
- A willingness to share, not hoard, information
- The foresight to acknowledge shared credit for achievements

Candidates who appear highly qualified in education, experience, and technical skills can quickly become disruptive influences if they are combative or negative. Perhaps these candidates are available because they didn't fit in with their previous or current employer. What will be different in your environment?

This factor also emphasizes the stake your current employees have in your hiring decisions. You may hire *Attila the candidate* who creates turmoil with your people. With one ill-advised hire, you could create several new vacancies and lose people you didn't want to lose. You are not hiring for one job, you are hiring for environmental health as well.

For many managers, preserving the health of the work environment is a significant challenge because it means hiring people who are considered different. Wise managers seek candidates who can offset their own weaknesses as well as those of the group, team, or departmental status quo. Effective managers hire with the intention of developing candidates to replace them!

Hiring Assessment Exercise

Step One: List the names of three individuals you have worked for, worked with, or employed whom you consider exceptional performers. These are the superstars you have worked with in your career. Identify a minimum of five skills that helped to define his or her greatness.

Step Two: Evaluate the skills you have listed; were they educational, experience-related, technical, motivational, organizational, interactive, or chemistry/teamwork-based?

Step Three: Evaluate your responses. Of your fifteen minimum responses, which area of assessment was most dominant?

Step Four: Identify three additional individuals you have worked with who were poor performers (the type of employee you want to *refrain* from hiring). Identify a minimum of five weaknesses that define each employee's poor performance or disruptive behavior.

Step Five: Identify the skills the employees lacked that contributed to their negative performances.

Step Six: Identify which area of assessment is relevant: educational, experience-related, technical, motivational, organizational, interactive, or chemistry/teamwork-based.

Step Seven: Evaluate your responses. Do you see a trend? Are the areas of assessment that most identified weakness the same areas of assessment that most identified greatness?

What can you learn from this exercise?

In Chapter 3, we will begin to look at the challenges of finding the candidates who possess the most desirable skills.

Recruiting: Networking and Accessing Today's Hiring Pools

The second and third aspects of the planning phase of your quest to find, hire, and keep peak-performing employees are

- Identifying where you can find the people you want to attract to your organization
- Discovering what will make these attractive candidates respond positively to you and your organization

Recruiting

As a frontline manager, you are constantly recruiting. Although the human resources department may do much of the initial formal recruiting on an as-needed basis, you are the catalyst of all recruiting activity. It is unwise for frontline managers to ignore the importance of their recruiting efforts. As you live and die on the performance of your people, you must be vigilant in finding the best possible candidates to help you achieve your goals in today's workplace. Peak performers do *not* just miraculously walk through the front door. Recruiting is too important a task to be done sporadically or to be left in the hands of others, no matter how competent.

In this chapter we will discuss many aspects of the recruiting process. Truth be told, you may not have much influence within your organization on many of these items. If you have direct influence or control, exercise it. If you do not, at least use every opportunity to make recommendations. Regardless of your circumstance, sharpen your awareness and knowledge of all the recruiting options, because things change dramatically in today's workplace. What you have little or no influence over today may become one of your primary responsibilities tomorrow.

The most important rule of effective recruiting is to develop as many avenues as possible to reach out to perspective candidates. You cannot rely on just a few methods. In the past, you could run one newspaper ad and a multitude of good candidates would break down the door in their desire to work for you. Those days are over.

John Korzec of Otis Elevator Company commented:

The key to good recruiting is to be tapped into a lot of different candidate pools. You must know how to write effective ads, you need to advertise in trade magazines periodically, you have to identify and develop a rapport with a few good recruiters, and you cannot avoid being on the Internet. The key is to be tapped into multiple pools as opposed to just one area. I don't think there is just one great recruiting idea that will suddenly meet all of your needs. You have to have a multifaceted approach to recruiting and you have to constantly adjust and tweak it. There is no silver bullet and you cannot rely on just one source to get it done.

When you have established your needs assessment and identified the skill sets your candidates must possess, ask yourself this question:

Where are the best candidates likely to be and how do I
find them?

It is important to target your recruiting efforts in areas where you will have access to the best candidates and high likelihood exists that those candidates will have an interest in joining your organization.

Terry Luck is a Regional Vice President with Nationwide Advertising Service, a human resources recruitment agency specializing in recruitment advertising. His agency writes, designs, and places recruitment advertisements for companies that are trying to attract high-quality candidates. The company also offers preemployment background checks, direct mail pieces, brochures, pamphlets, flyers, and structured employee referral programs.

Terry offered his thoughts on targeting your recruiting efforts:

If you are looking for orange growers, where would you actively recruit to hire them? Obviously, you would target southern California and probably Florida. Why? Because you know that's where the people are with the background you are looking for. However, a lot of companies will actually recruit heavily in a city just because it's a larger area or because other organizations and other managers have had success running ads there. However, it is highly possible that with the appropriate planning or professional guidance, you may discover there are areas with much greater potential. Perhaps there are seven companies in another area, only two and a half hours down the road from you, that may be reorganizing or laying off the exact types of candidates you seek. Rather than running a national ad or ads only in your largest city, it may be in your best interest to target a specific market, and those markets continuously change. It may be wise to increase your efforts in an area that has four, five, or six of your direct competitors, as well as other companies that you could potentially hire from. Unfortunately, many frontline managers, because they have so many things on their plate, will just not have the knowledge or experience or expertise to know where to look. So the path of least resistance is to go to your local newspaper, call the advertising desk, and leave your recruiting in the hands of the help-wanted department. I think they are really shortchanging themselves by doing that.

Recruiting is an expensive task. You want to invest wisely in your efforts. Pursuing unfertile areas can waste significant dollars; effective recruiting can be conducted cost effectively if it is well planned.

One successful recruiting strategy is to recruit within eight hours (or five hundred miles) of your location. Many people are willing to relocate within a day's drive from their homes, and in our mobile society, relocation is frequently not a major impediment to accepting a new position. In the past, people expected to seek and accept employment within a short distance of their traditional homes. Today, that expectation is the exception, not the rule. Relocation costs are obviously a factor to consider when recruiting; however, the upfront cost of relocation can be a relatively small price to pay for finding peak-performing candidates. Consider all the possible recruiting pools within the eight-hour target area; this does not mean that a broader-based search is never called for, but it is often best to start close to home.

Another recruiting factor that is frequently overlooked is the importance of the spouse, significant other, parents, or anyone else who may be a part of a candidate's support system. When you hire candidates, others may have a great stake in their accepting or rejecting your job offer. It is common for candidates to seek opinions from those closest to them and give great weight to their input. The influence from others can, in some instances, make or break your recruiting efforts. Do everything possible to include these other sources of influence appropriately in the recruiting and hiring process. For your comfort and that of the candidates, provide these significant influencers with

- Information concerning the organization, especially emphasizing benefits packages
- List of current employees with similar backgrounds to whom they can turn for references on you and the organization
- The opportunity to participate in segments of the interviewing process (especially when the candidate is interviewing *you*)
- Help in seeking new employment if relocation is involved and they are a part of the move
- Details of local services, schools, and healthcare providers if relocation is required

Even if your influence over recruiting efforts is minimal, you probably do have significant influence in these four aspects of recruiting:

Networking   Employee referrals
Internal searches   Monitoring current
                       economic events

Networking

In the past when someone became unemployed, it was considered a negative, sometimes shameful circumstance, and people took great pains to hide the information from others. Too often, a negative social stigma was attached to being unemployed. If someone is without a job today, the first thing that person is encouraged to do is network! People are encouraged to make others aware of their circumstances and to seek help through referrals and recommendations. Today, instead of suppressing the information, people are eager to shout it out and share it with as many people as possible. To be an effective recruiter, you have to become a part of the mainstream network. You must place the same emphasis on networking to find employees as they are placing on finding employment. Plug into the network!

The more people who are aware of your need to hire peak performers, the better your recruiting efforts will be. Your networking activities should never cease. Become known as a reference point that people can use when they learn of others who may be seeking employment. Do not expect this to be a one-time activity; you must constantly be renewing and replenishing your network sources. Telling someone today that you are interested in hiring peak-performing candidates does not ensure that the contact will refer someone to you ninety days from now. Most people will probably assume that your position is no longer available and your interest in hiring someone has waned, which is *never* the case.

Networking equals activity, and the sources for your efforts may typically include

- Participation in professional associations (either as a

member or a sponsor, including those whose members possess transferable skills. Do not limit your activity only to those associations directly related to your industry or specific profession.)

- Support of alumni associations
- Membership in civic associations (chamber of commerce, noncontroversial political groups, school associations, and so on. A great source of referrals can be the children of other members, recent college graduates, and so forth.)
- Visibility in local gathering places (health clubs, sporting events, homeowners associations)

When you receive a referral through your network, it is important to

- Formally acknowledge the referring individual with a statement of thanks (a note, e-mail, phone message, and so on)
- Emphasize with the potential candidate how much you appreciate and value the referring individual
- Treat potential candidates well even if you do not have any interest in them (if candidates believe they were treated badly or just "blown off," they will communicate that information back to the referring individual and you will never receive that person's help again)
- When you do not have an interest, refer the candidate to others, if possible
- Offer a formal "thank you" to the referring individual if you do hire the candidate (dinner for two is a great expression of your appreciation)

Internal Searches

Perhaps the most obvious place to look for candidates is elsewhere within your organization. If you are a small business concern, this may not be an option; often, however, and especially in medium to large companies, highly attractive candidates can be found elsewhere in the organization. It is extremely advantageous for you to be able to offer upward mobility to your internal people. Demonstrating and documenting that employees who are successful in one area are given either promotion or attractive lateral moves into other areas of choice can be an important part of your retention efforts. If your employees believe they must leave the organization to move up, employee longevity is negatively affected.

The obvious downside to the organization is that moving an exceptional performer from one area to another merely transfers the vacancy. Although it may solve your current recruiting problem, it creates the same problem for another manager. Because of this, the overall organizational benefit must be considered; however, to deny employees positive internal movement consistently is not necessarily a sign of a healthy, vibrant organization. Also keep in mind that you must anticipate and support opportunities for the internal movement of your own people. (Another good reason for you to be constantly vigilant in your networking and recruiting efforts is that you never know when a vacancy will occur.) You cannot take employees from others if you are not willing to participate yourself. You must also focus consistently on what is best for present employees.

Employee Referrals

Your best source of recruiting may well be your current peak-performing employees. Typically, the tentacles of their networks and associations run deep. They may know and have intimate knowledge of the exceptional performers through their peers in other organizations, their friends within the local community, or their classmates in college; and through military connections and relationships with members of professional and civic organizations. They may be more "plugged in" to these recruiting sources than you.

Hunter Johnson is the Director of Human Resources at World Strides in Charlottesville, Virginia. World Strides is the largest student-education-related travel company in the United States; the company coordinates over 200,000 students every year for educational travel. Hunter is enthusiastic about his employees' referrals of others for employment:

> Current employees are my best recruiters. If they really enjoy working here and they like being a part of our organization, they tell their friends and other people they interact with, who are generally competent people like themselves. This has been very effective for us. The upside is, I get a lot of great candidates. As a matter of fact, people are frequently calling us saying, "I hear World Strides is a great place to work and if there's any openings, I would be like to hear about them because I'm not happy where I'm working and I'm looking for a change." This produces a great stream of very good potential employees.

One significant advantage to encouraging referrals from current employees is that they help pick the people they work with; this usually stimulates collaboration and a positive work environment (stressing the importance of chemistry, teamwork, and collaboration, as we discussed in Chapter 2). Employees who recommend others also have a stake in the success of the people they recommend. They tend to offer more encouragement to their new employee referrals and are usually willing to augment and support your training efforts to ensure their referrals' success.

To encourage employee referrals, many organizations offer a bonus or an incentive to those who recommend a candidate who is hired. It is to your advantage to tie incentive to longevity whenever possible. Offer incremental payoffs, perhaps on the first day the new employee starts, once again on the employee's six-month anniversary, with the largest amount being offered if the recommended employee is still with you after one year. This gives the referring employees reason to be extra supportive and to encourage their referrals to stay.

Use your creativity when offering incentives. It is probably best to structure the incentives to escalate in value as the new employee's time of service lengthens. The first payoff could be as simple as dinner for four at a local restaurant, paid for by the company. This allows current employees and their referrals to celebrate with their spouses, significant others, and so on. Cash bonuses can be offered at the six- and twelve-month intervals; however, other incentives may work as effectively. Consider

- Purchasing frequent flyer miles for referring employees (or offering them free round-trip tickets to destinations of their choice)
- Additional paid vacation days (on a one-time basis during the referral year, *not* ongoing)
- A three-to-five-day getaway vacation at company expense at a local resort or attraction
- Tickets to Disneyland or Disney World! (This never hurts.)

Although cash is always welcome, you can usually obtain a bigger payoff from alternative incentives, especially those that allow the referring employee to share the incentive with others (family, friends, and so on). Cash is impersonal; other incentives can be more inclusive. This offers referring employees the opportunity to share their bounty with others who are important to them. This has multiple payoffs. If spouse, Mom, Dad, or friend is awarded something that they can share with others, they receive positive recognition from those closest to them as well as the goodwill of having helped someone else find new employment and a career opportunity.

Cash bonuses, if necessary, can be in the form of preestablished amounts or a percentage of the new employee's salary. It may also be effective to allow the referring employee to receive a percentage of the new employee's first year performance bonus if one is earned.

There are downsides to employee referral programs. The first is that you run the risk of creating an unintended lack of organizational diversity. It is natural for employees to recommend people who are just like themselves. If you already have a diverse workforce that reflects a healthy integration of skill levels, age, gender, race, culture, and so on, you probably won't have a diversity problem with employee referrals. If your current diversity is limited, however, beware of expanding the limited dimension of your workforce.

Another downside is the potential for discipline and morale problems. If you find it necessary to confront or discipline employees concerning performance or behavior problems, they usually share their unhappiness with their closest associates. Instead of having one unhappy employee, you now have at least two. This situation is especially troublesome in hiring family members; it is one of the reasons many organizations have restrictions limiting the employment of people who are related. As with most things in life, there are upsides and downsides to everything. In general, the positives of employee referral programs vastly outweigh inherent negatives.

Monitor Current Economic Events

Information is readily available concerning trends in your industry, as well as in the overall economy. Recruiting opportunities may surface in your area, especially concerning organizations that are downsizing, restructuring, or experiencing mergers and acquisitions. In many of these circumstances, exceptional performers may be losing their jobs through no fault of their own. These events are generally announced in advance; it is to your advantage to contact the involved organization's human resources department directly if you believe that any of their employees could be a match for you and your organization. When these major changes and disruptions occur, the involved organization usually has a strong internal desire to help its employees find new opportunities and makes concentrated efforts on their behalf. You will be welcomed with open arms, especially if you can be flexible in your hiring plans. If unionized workers are involved, it is also appropriate to make direct contact with local union officials.

If you can allow potential employees to finish a commitment with their current employers, and then offer them a quick transition into your organization, you will probably experience great cooperation. To protect their remaining productivity, some organizations discourage employees from leaving early when a downsizing, merger, or closing is announced. Be sensitive to this issue when contacting potential candidates or their current organization.

Tom Trotter is the General Manager of Howmet Castings in LaPorte, Indiana. Howmet is the world's leading producer of castings and finished components for the aerospace and industrial power generation markets. A division of the Alcoa Corporation, Howmet employs 10,000 people worldwide. Tom shared his thoughts on networking, internal searches, and the monitoring of current economic events:

There have been a couple of recruiting strategies we have been extremely successful with recently. One is networking like crazy. For example, I had a particular position that I wanted to fill on the staff here. I started calling around to my peers in other organizations, asking them if they had any suggestions for good people. I ended up receiving a couple of excellent referrals of people who were very capable and respected in their field. We were able to find an excellent candidate to accept the position, and this was just from networking efforts. I've also done the same thing on the inside of Howmet. When I've had a position to fill, I talked to several other plant managers to come up with a couple of very good referrals, and many of those folks are now working here. The key to networking is to target the kind of person you are looking for and find sources who might know people like that, and then it's just a matter of getting on the phone. We do have quite a bit of involvement with professional associations and some of our people have good connections with alumni associates. We also keep an eye out for mergers and acquisitions. When Honeywell and Allied Signal merged, we knew there would be a fallout of some good people who were just caught in the middle. We were able to target this, and through the use of a recruiter, we were able to contact excellent candidates who were victims of the change affecting those organizations. As a result of that particular merger and acquisition, we were able to get a quality manager who is a real change agent and has been an excellent addition to our staff. So keeping an eye out for those kinds of circumstances presents opportunities for increased exceptional staffing. There is also a plant in Michigan City, Indiana, not too far from us, that is getting ready to close. We've gone directly to their H.R. director and he has provided us with names of people who may be able to fill our needs. Most H.R. professionals are very interested in helping their people find a job someplace else.

Traditional Recruiting Pools

Obviously, your recruiting efforts should include, but not be limited to, the continued use of the traditional recruiting sources. These resources are generally considered to be

Professional recruiters	State or public job services
College recruiting	Newspaper and print
Student internships	media advertising

It is always wise to vary your approach, not becoming dependent on any one traditional recruiting source. If used properly, these sources can continue to be an important part of your recruiting effort and yield peak-performing candidates.

Newspaper and Print Media Advertising

By far the most traditional method for attracting candidates. In recent years, advertising has not always generated the flood of peak-performing exceptional candidates that it has in the past; however, it is unwise to abandon this avenue completely. Rethinking the appeal of your ads and targeting your activity in specific newspapers and journals can continue to yield results.

The dominant newspaper in the largest city closest to your location is the first consideration for print advertising. You must also consider national publications and local or regional newspapers. Always keep in mind the job you are advertising and the candidates you wish to attract. What publications are those candidates likely to read? If relocation is a negative, do not advertise in print media that is published outside of your general location. If you are looking for candidates with specific experience, target print media such as professional journals and trade magazines that enjoy a high readership in that industry.

Assess your ads to determine their appeal. Will they attract the attention of potential candidates and encourage them to contact you?

Terry Luck, who has strong expertise in the print market arena, said:

> There are really three things that attract people's attention in recruitment advertising. Size, in other words how big the ad is. Next is some type of graphic or illustration, perhaps including the use of a photograph. Third is the use of color. If you can make people stop and look at your ad, basically 50 percent of the job has already been done. Then you have to be able to tell them something in either a subheading or an introductory paragraph that will entice them to read more, and then provide the contact information so they, hopefully, will initiate an action and contact you.

Cost is always an issue in using the print media, and smaller ads that draw a smaller but higher quality response may be more cost-effective than a full-page ad. If you do not use the services of an advertising specialist, it is important to review the ads that are currently running in the newspapers you select to be sure that yours is somehow distinctive. Do not run the same ad repetitively in the same newspapers. Ads get old, and candidates seeing the same placement begin to draw negative conclusions and probably won't respond.

In today's job market, people want specific information from the ads they review.

Avoid generalized phrases that can be perceived as "come-ons" or driven by emotional hype. Identify job *reality* versus job *potential*. Avoid such phrases as "Wanted, highly motivated self-starter interested in six-figure income." Today's high-quality candidates are not responding to smoke and mirrors.

Headline your ad with an accurate descriptive title and a brief summary of the job description. Emphasize the aspects of the job that are most rewarding and appealing. Also emphasize the benefits the job brings, including health care, 401(k), vacation, and stock options, and the realistic pathway for growth and advancement. If you can honestly make a statement such as, "The position is available because the current staff member has been promoted after eighteen months on the job," this would appeal to candidates seeking upward mobility.

Also state clearly the conditions for response. How to contact you: phone, fax, or e-mail, whether you request an initial resume, and the appropriate days and times, if necessary. Clearly identifying your organization and naming a specific contact person in the ad is generally more effective than expecting people to respond to a blind post office box.

Targeting specific trade journals for print media advertising can be very successful. Terry Luck:

> If XYZ Engineering Company was looking for a construction industry design engineer, we would recommend running an ad in the local market as well as regional newspapers. We would also recommend utilization of industry-specific trade journals, especially geared to design engineers that have a construction background. This would be particularly important if attracting

these types of candidates was an ongoing need. These journals represent a captive audience. People subscribe to them because they have a genuine interest in the journal content. Publications that people actually pay for are much more effective than those they receive as part of a general distribution mailing for free.

Another nontraditional aspect of print media is the use of billboards. They tend to be affordable and give you visibility for a minimum of thirty days. Nothing ventured. nothing gained!

College Recruiting

Although highly competitive, effective college recruiting can yield impressive results. Traditionally dominated by large big-name organizations, this candidate pool is open to organizations of any size. It is best to target your recruiting to schools in which people from your area are enrolled (local students go to many institutions; however, usually a couple of "hot schools of the moment" attract a larger percentage of locals) and that graduate candidates you have an interest in interviewing.

When pursuing college recruiting, you are attracting younger candidates who are short on experience; however, many demonstrate high ambition, energy, and intellect. They are also in tune with the learning process and tend to be open to training. One downside is their high mobility, and it is not uncommon for the first job they accept after graduation to have a short duration; because of this, tremendous pressure will be exerted on your managerial skills to maintain retention.

Butch Krishnamurti works for John Korzec as the Manager of Human Resources for Otis Elevator Company in Bloomington, Indiana. His responsibilities are those of a human resource generalist; he oversees activities in support of salaried staff, which includes plant recruiting, training, and salary administration. Butch is a college recruiting specialist. He shared these comments concerning his college recruiting efforts:

College recruiting is definitely a pretty big part of our recruiting strategy. Many of the positions we have recruited for are considered entry-level professional positions, and we often target college students soon to receive a degree to fill these types of positions. In these entry-level positions we do not necessarily need a seasoned candidate who brings with them a lot of previous work experience. Instead, we may concentrate on finding students who attend good higher-learning institutions and who demonstrate through school experience or otherwise competencies we seek for these position openings. We are fortunate to have some very good colleges in our local area, including Indiana University and Purdue University.

Butch added a cautionary note:

One downside is that if you need a specialized skill, even if it's at an entry-level position, you may not find it through college recruiting. However, even in these circumstances you may find some students who did receive some related experience through summer internships or work-related study programs, and, therefore, may still meet your position requirements.

Preparation is important in maximizing your college recruiting efforts. Butch added,

The most important thing to make sure you have a successful recruiting trip is to have a clear understanding of what it is specifically that you are looking for. What I have found, particularly in people who are not well trained in interviewing, is that they sometimes have not prepared enough up front to understand the specific needs of the company. By this I mean knowing what specific positions the company needs and what knowledge, skills, and abilities each position requires. This should all be done before a recruiting effort commences to ensure the right colleges and students are targeted via your recruiting effort.

Typically, college recruiting has been done through the human resources office, and smaller organizations without a formal human resources recruiting support have not pursued this activity. If your organization is not targeting the college recruiting pool, it is one you might consider, regardless of your size. You may want to start with local colleges and institutions in your area. Small companies can do well, although it is a competitive environment. Your compensation and benefit packages must be consistent with those in your industry, and hiring incentives may be necessary to attract the best and brightest.

If your organization is currently pursuing college talent, it is important that you routinely send different people to conduct the recruiting to ensure diversity. There is also great advantage for you, as a frontline manager, to participate in these efforts. Students place great value on talking to the person for whom they will be working directly; they can gain a competitive edge, especially if you participate early in the recruiting process. In many recruiting circumstances, candidates do not meet their potential new bosses until the end of the hiring process.

To initiate a college recruitment effort, contact the placement office of the appropriate department whose graduates you wish to consider. Schools are eager for you to pursue their students. College recruiting is in everyone's best interest.

Butch shared these observations:

Colleges are very receptive. Most of the schools are really in the business of trying to recruit companies to come on campus and they are usually very excited by your interest. However, I will tell you, depending on the school's popularity and the notoriety of their departments, you can have a very difficult time getting a schedule if you don't allow proper lead time. For example, the fall tends to be the heaviest time to do interviews, usually from September through December. You may have to act as early as six months in advance to make sure your organization gets a slot. If you don't reserve well in advance, you may find your desired dates are unavailable. Again, the interview schedules begin to fill very quickly. In some two-year community colleges or technical schools, you may not have quite the same lead-time issues, but advance booking in these cases is still highly recommended.

As far as contacting colleges to begin the process, Butch said:

Almost all colleges and universities have a placement center, and this is a good first point of contact. In fact, some colleges even have a separate placement center for different programs of study on campus. For example, at Indiana University,, the Business School has its own placement center while some of the programs belong to another placement center. Both centers are located on the Bloomington campus. I have found that placement centers are generally very helpful in helping me devise an effective recruiting plan for that campus. Things I usually need to know include what interview schedules are still available, how do I provide information about our company and open positions to prospective interested students on campus, do I need to preselect students to be on the interview schedule, or is there an open bidding system, and what logistical information do I need regarding my on-campus visit to conduct the interviews. The placement centers typically have all this information readily available to convey to company representatives and usually help in whatever way necessary to help me in having a good recruiting experience at their school

When you contact the placement centers you will find many have policies for on-campus recruiting, including:

- Proof of legitimate business licensing must be offered.
- Candidates must have a minimum of three weeks to consider a job offer.
- Compensation can be presented only as guaranteed; commissions, bonuses, and incentives must be clearly identified and not used to entice unfairly.

For the most part, you will find the schools easy and willing to do business.

Student Internships

Traditionally, the realm of larger organizations, internships can be established by organizations of any size through colleges, universities, and trade schools. Contacting individual departments at the school and presenting your proposal can yield great potential employment candidates. This strategy offers you the opportunity to experience the quality of their work, work ethics, and to build solid relationships for offering interns permanent future employment. Schools are interested in providing internship opportunities for their students, and in many cases the students earn credit for work that meets class requirements. Internships can be a win-win situation for your organization, the school, and the student.

John Korzec on internships:

We have an intern/co-op program where we will bring in 25–30 candidates from various schools every year and then some of these folks will become full-time employees. It's also important to the college recruiting effort to have a good intern/co-op program. Our program is predominantly focused on summer employment, although we do have a co-op program year round where people will work at Otis. Ideally we would like to contact an individual at the end of their first or second year of college and bring them back for a couple of years. We can establish a relationship and rapport with the candidate and be the first company to extend a job offer. We have found this to be very successful.

You may not be able to provide twenty-five or thirty internships; however, perhaps you can provide one.

Professional Recruiters

These organizations range from professional- and executive-level search firms to employment agencies to temporary support providers.

Professional recruiters receive fees for their services, whether they represent the candidate or the client organization. Fees are established through set revenue schedules and are collected from candidates, client companies, or both. Candidate-paid fees are rapidly disappearing. Some fees are based on percentages of starting salary, either on a one-time basis or collectively over years. These firms can also establish retainer fees for client companies and may include expanded employment services.

Employment agencies generally provide candidates for administrative and support staff positions, whereas professional executive recruiters tend to focus on entry, midlevel, and executive management and leadership positions. It is important to establish a good relationship with the professional recruiters you use; they can provide excellent candidates and save you a lot of time and effort. The downside is that some may send you warm bodies. They "guarantee" their placements by providing replacement candidates if their referrals do not work out; but this can result in a parade of marginal candidates, the recruiter hoping that one will stick. Rarely do professional recruiters want to refund your money. Fees and terms are negotiable. Select wisely; the good ones can be very good.

Art Lucas is President and CEO. of The Lucas Group, a thirty-year-old professional recruiting search firm, headquartered in Atlanta, Georgia. The firm has offices in eleven cities and focuses on placing candidates in thirty-four niche professions and job categories. When asked about the advantages of using a professional firm, Art had these comments:

The biggest advantage of firms such as ours is that we can usually find talent faster and better than our client organizations. That's our business. We live and sleep this business, twenty-four hours a day, seven days a week. Our job is to go out and do what I call "pinpoint recruiting." A client tells us exactly what they want to hire, and we go find it for them. They may want someone who speaks Spanish, has some unique experience in the marketplace, perhaps leadership skills or a specific technical expertise, and they may not be easy to find. Usually these people are successfully working for a competitor, and it's very difficult for one of our client companies to go in to a competitor and recruit an employee. That's what we do. We go to Company B and approach the candidate who has all the skill sets that Company A is looking for. This is a unique skill. Recruiting top people is not an easy thing to do, especially in this economy. We can contact the candidate, entice them to talk to the potential new employer, assist in negotiating the offer, and help the candidate and their new organization build a good relationship. That's why people use professional firms. Sometimes when you put an ad in the paper, you get the raging masses, and you may not get the person you're looking for. Most of the people we place aren't actually looking. They are the passive job-seekers. We bring opportunities to them. That's the primary value of a professional firm such as ours.

In the past, temporary agencies focused primarily on providing the services of hourly employees, such as manufacturing, delivery, or warehouse personnel, including some office and clerical workers. Recently, many temporary agencies have become specialized in providing short-term contract help with professional experience, training, and backgrounds. Numerous organizations have found a "temporary-to-permanent job program" helpful in hiring peak performers. Employees are initially provided by a temporary agency on a contract basis, and if an employee's performance meets or exceeds expectations, he or she can be offered permanent employment, generally within a range of ninety days to one year. The agency receives a fee for permanent placements, much as a professional recruiter does. The advantage is that you *see* before you *buy*. If the employee's performance is not acceptable during the temporary placement, another candidate is found and the organization is not obligated in any way.

The temporary-to-permanent hiring process has downsides. Perhaps most glaring is the serious negative factor it presents to currently employed candidates who may have an interest in joining your organization. Most are unwilling to risk temporary employment when they are currently in a secure permanent position. The candidate is asked not only to take a risk but to compromise eligibility for vacation, sick days, and so forth (some of the things you can negotiate as hiring incentives, which we will discuss in later chapters). However, temporary agencies are an option worth considering as a piece of your recruiting puzzle.

State and Public Job Services

You will find state, federally, and privately funded job placement entities within your area. People are required to register with these job bureaus to receive training or financial assistance supported by public or private funds. In the past, candidates generated by these sources have, at times, been viewed with unnecessary skepticism, and these bureaus have been unfairly maligned. Include these services in your overall recruiting efforts. A candidate generated from these resources can be as valuable as any other. These services are especially valuable during times of economic slowdown. Leave no stone unturned.

Nontraditional Recruiting Pools

Although some of these pools are rapidly becoming commonplace, they represent previously unrecognized or untapped reservoirs of potentially peak-performing employees. In many cases, nontraditional recruiting pools require you to reevaluate your traditional thinking concerning what defines attractive employment candidates. Many great peak performers are being found in previously uncharted waters.

World Wide Web Resources

Internet advertising, job posting boards, and direct links to search engines make the Internet a valuable resource for recruiting certain candidates. People searching for technically oriented positions are more apt to search the Web than others, and not every position you wish to fill will attract an Internet-savvy candidate. The World Wide Web is obviously here to stay; however, it is *not* a magic recruiting bullet.

Terry Luck had this comment:

> In the last four or five years, the Internet has really had an impact on our business. We view the Internet as an additional resource, just like we would a trade publication or a newspaper. When we do an actual recruiting plan for a company, we also include Internet advertising as part of the media mix, along with newspaper ads, brochures, trade publications, and so on. Some of our competitors feel the Internet is going to take over and other print media is going to go away. At Nationwide Advertising we do not feel that way. We do believe the Internet is going to play an increased role, but we believe that print media will always be here. Obviously, some of the younger generation, usually referred to as Generation-X, have grown up on computers and the Internet, and its usage is becoming very widespread. It must be a part of everyone's recruiting efforts.

Your Internet strategy should be twofold: attracting candidates to your organization or Web site through the use of advertising and/or job boards. You can also access sites where resumes are posted. Searching keywords associated with your industry can generally begin a successful search.

Please keep in mind that even with the attraction and availability of the Web, the majority of employees still do not have access to personal computers or the inclination to use the computer as a job-search tool; this situation is changing, however, as more people every day purchase and use personal computers. In general, the higher the education level and the greater the past employment responsibility, the greater the likelihood a candidate will use the Internet as a tool. The Internet is not a cure-all for recruiting and hiring; however, it should be a valuable part of your efforts.

Military Resources

People retiring or exiting from the military can be excellent candidates. Almost all bring exceptional training, technical skills, and discipline to the workplace.

Mike Devereaux is Vice President of the Lucas Group's Military Division. He is located in Dallas, Texas, and is responsible for a sixty-person group that places junior military mid-level officers and noncommissioned officers into the corporate world. When asked about the advantages of considering military candidates for employment, Mike responded:

I think the number one attribute of military candidates is leadership. We refer to them as developmental candidates and they are people who can enter an organization and can either start in and/or develop into leadership positions in a short period of time. A lot of organizations are starving for leadership and these candidates can provide it. The second key attribute is loyalty. We have a track record to measure, and as long as you take care of military candidates, they will tend to stay with an organization. Eighty-five percent of our placements stay with their organization five years or more. And to a degree, that's bucking the trend in many industries. Another important thing is, they get the job done. They are used to working fourteen- to sixteen-hour days, different shifts, Saturdays and Sundays, and many times on twenty-four-hour operations. They are very goal-oriented. They are also people who are used to getting the job done without complaining. The bottom line is, they are promotable, and that's what organizations are looking for.

As with all potential candidates, there can be some downsides to hiring candidates from the military. In general, candidates from the military are accustomed to a structured environment and are used to following instructions; in many cases, they are used to having their instructions followed to the letter. Unfortunately, in many organizations, the environment is not that responsive. Military candidates can require an adjustment period so that they can become acclimatized to the civilian workplace. The pace of change, too, especially in smaller entrepreneurial operations, may challenge the flexibility and adaptability of some of these candidates. However, when balanced against the experience, training, and performance potential of military-related candidates, the downsides are secondary.

Diverse-Profile Candidates

The potential of many groups has been relatively untapped in the past. Some of these groups are finding themselves in great demand in today's workplace. Many are seeking employment; some are passive resources just waiting to be tapped.

Experienced Workers (Fifty-Five and Older). Many are retired with excellent experience from their previous careers. Some wish to generate earnings to support their current incomes; others seek the challenge of continued employment. Although they may not provide exceptionally long-term service to your organization, they can give a minimum of three to five years of productivity (about the average length of younger employees' time of service).

Physically Disabled. The explosion of technology is one example of how many of today's critical jobs can be performed by people whose disabilities might have prevented them from performing in past circumstances. Disabled workers can provide valuable productivity at all organizational levels. Assess your opportunities for the possibility of hiring a peak performer with physical limitations.

Foreign Workers. Usually legal foreigners are highly skilled and in demand. Information technology environments, healthcare, and some service industries are examples of groups who find this pool of candidates attractive. They can be a tremendous source of skilled, highly performing employees.

Part-Timers and Job Sharers. Many people are choosing to limit their involvement in the workplace for reasons concerning quality of life. Instead of hiring one full-time person, it may be advantageous to restructure the job and hire two people possessing the skills to accomplish the tasks. Many women, wishing to spend more time at home with their children, are pursuing reduced-hour job-sharing opportunities. You can find many who were previously employed in significant jobs willing to accept responsibilities on a limited time basis. Many retired or older workers fall into this category.

Gaining access to the people who may constitute these and other nontraditional groups can be a challenge. All the strategies we have discussed so far will be helpful. Many candidates will surface through your networking efforts, and it would be to your advantage to consider these alternatives.

Job Networking and Employment Support Groups

Many candidates of all backgrounds turn to a structured support group in times of unemployment, especially those with stable backgrounds who find being out of a job an unusual and challenging experience. Job network and support groups provide training in effective job searching, résumé writing, and interviewing, along with positive encouragement. Many have a religious sponsorship; however, they are generally open to all. Listings are provided in most major newspapers for these groups, who meet in various locations throughout all major cities. Attending a session or contacting the group leader can bring a wealth of highly qualified candidates. You may even be given the opportunity to speak to the groups about job searches, industry trends, interviewing skills, and so forth.

Maintaining a Network of Contacts Within
Religious Organizations

The demands on your time probably dictate that you limit this contact to the largest religious groups in your area, for example, major churches, synagogues, mosques, temples, and so forth. When people find themselves unemployed, they often search for spiritual guidance. Letting the clergy or leaders of these groups know your ongoing interest in hiring high-quality peak-performing people gives them information they can pass along to their members. Generally, it is important to keep this network open, and a quarterly contact, e-mail, or phone call keeps your contact active. Many religious groups maintain a formal internal referral bank for job opportunities, and your networking will provide you with contact information.

Community and Church Publications

Although having a limited circulation, these can be an excellent nontraditional source for reaching peak performers. One CEO we talked to told us that when she was looking for an upper-level manager, she put notices in several upscale homeowners' association newsletters. The position she was offering had a salary in excess of $80,000 a year, and she reasoned that highly compensated people would live in these areas and have access to her information. She received several inquiries from highly qualified individuals. She said, "I thought it was worth looking in areas where my ideal candidate might live." Apparently, she was right.

Local Gathering Places

Senior centers, recreation departments, malls where walking clubs meet, as well as health clubs, golf course clubhouses, and various local volunteer organizations—all have access to people who may be qualified, have an interest in your position, and have been untapped in the past. Many gathering places have directors who can share information, bulletin boards for posting information, and informal internal networks for getting the word out.

Finding qualified candidates is not an easy task. Your creativity will serve you well.

Recruiting Assessment Exercise

Step One: What traditional recruiting methods have served you and your organization well in the past?

- Are these still valid?

- Should their use be increased or decreased?
- What changes, if any, should be made in your approach?

Step Two: What nontraditional methods or recruiting pools may have the best payoff for your organization?

- How can you begin to penetrate this area?
- Who else within your organization can be helpful in planning or using this approach?

Step Three: What other creative opportunities, perhaps not mentioned in this chapter, do you have for finding peak-performing candidates?

4

Preparing for the Interview

The final point in the planning phase is preparing to interview the candidates you have found. In this chapter, we will discuss

- The value of resumes
- The proper use of phone screening
- Interview logistics

The Value of Resumes

Resumes are curious tools. Most serious job candidates value them highly and many take great pains to produce what amounts to a slick piece of advertising copy. Many people hope that somehow their resumes will literally reach out and grab their next employers and demand that they be hired. Everyone wants to believe that somehow his or her resume is magically different.

In theory, a resume is a factual statement of a candidate's education, experience, and workplace skills. In reality, this information is often generously intertwined with fantasy and fiction. To varying degrees, resumes are subjected to a candidates' distorted and embellished views of themselves and reality. Some resumes contain outright lies; most contain exaggerated truths. Perhaps we shouldn't judge candidates and their resumes too harshly. Truth be known, if you or I really wanted or needed a specific job, we might be tempted to embellish a little, too! Can you imagine receiving a resume that says, "I am a mediocre performer with a horrible work ethic who gets bored easy and probably won't stay with you for more than four months. I also have real problems following rules and policies, but I hope you will hire me anyway"!

You are responsible, as a frontline manager, to remove the embellishments, exaggerations, or distortions surgically and discover a candidate's relevant experiences and skills.

In truth, most managers would rather spend eight hours in a dentist's chair than sit and read a stack of resumes. By reputation, resumes are considered, at best, suspect. They are usually viewed skeptically as documents riddled with exaggerations and inaccuracies. Many candidates see compiling a resume as an opportunity to create their own pedigrees.

Most resumes probably end up in the paper shredder. The use of resumes has evolved into a negative function, a tool to screen candidates *out* or to determine whom you *don't* want to interview. Because most recruiting efforts are based on narrow (and obsolete) job descriptions, resumes are soon discarded if they aren't a perfect match or don't contain the same specific language. Resumes are reviewed for exact matches on educational background and experience, and if this information is not there exactly as desired, the candidate is probably excluded from consideration. Typically, little or no attempt is made to read into the resume and find camouflaged opportunities.

Resumes have become the weapons of the gatekeepers. In their quest to find the perfect candidate on paper, untold numbers of talented imperfect candidates have been discarded and hordes of perfect candidates have crashed and burned in blazes of glorious rejection. For you, as a frontline manager, resumes are a valuable piece of the hiring process, to be neither over-valued nor underestimated.

Resumes should be used as tools of inclusion to screen in as many candidates as possible, not as scalpels to cut them out. Never allow a written document to deny you access to a potential peak performer unless it reflects an obvious and irreparable lack of qualifications.

As a frontline manager, resumes can be a valuable tool. To use resumes properly, you must understand how they can best serve you and then develop a system for effective evaluation. A resume serves two basic purposes: to determine whether the candidate has potential value as an addition to your organization, and to help you formulate an interview plan.

Systematically Evaluating Resumes

The first consideration for a resume you review is its overall appearance. Does it indicate that its creator invested appropriate effort in its preparation and presentation? Does it contain spelling errors? Is the content presented in a clear, concise manner? Is everything in the proper tense? Are columns and fonts aligned properly? In this day and age of technology and with the availability of professional resume writing services, there is no excuse for a sloppy or improperly prepared resume. A candidate submitting an unacceptable resume is guilty of either creating the perception of his low interest in seeking employment or is oblivious of how the hiring process works. Either situation undoubtedly portends future employment problems!

Next, turn your attention to the resume's stated objective. This is probably the document's least useful component. At best, a stated objective merely reflects a candidate's attempt to put in writing what he or she thinks you want to read. What do you expect the candidate to say?

- My objective is to escape my current employment as soon as possible?
- My objective is to be paid an enormous amount of money for doing as little work as possible?
- My objective is to con you into hiring someone as bad as I am?

For review, quickly scan the objective and determine whether it was written by someone with an IQ above the fat content of a grape! Determine whether it reflects an ability to communicate a clear, concise message, and move on. It doesn't have much value for you beyond that.

The Color-Coded Review System

The resume helps you to determine whether to interview a candidate and serves as a guideline for the interviewing questions you want to ask. To review resumes effectively, you must develop a system to ensure consistency. Here is a five-step process to help you create a meaningful resource from the candidate's resume. The best systems are always the most simple and all you need is a highlighter (any color) and two colored pens (any colors as long as they are red and blue!). Take great liberties in writing or marking all over the resume. A well-reviewed resume usually ends up looking like a bad road map! Although you are free to make notations on a resume, never do so with a formal job application. Applications are permanent documents; marks and notations could be questioned and your notations misunderstood, no matter how innocent or meaningless.

Step One: Highlight Relevant Information. *Highlight* education, skills, and work experiences that appear to relate favorably to the position you are trying to fill. Look carefully in this information for anything that may indicate transferable skill opportunities. In the interview, you will review the highlighted information to

- Affirm your perceptions of applicability or transferability
- Verify its legitimacy
- Identify opportunities to seek independent documentation through proof statements, references, and background checks

Educational claims and work experiences are readily verifiable. Telling candidates that you will perform an extensive background and reference check usually causes "information distorters" to bail out rather quickly. Be wary of educational claims concerning institutions you have never heard of. Just because you are not aware of a particular school, university, or institute does not mean that it does not exist; however, diploma mills do exist and they sell degrees and credentials. Trust everyone . . . but . . . cut the cards! Always verify educational claims.

If candidates list company, association, or industry certifications, highlight these and ask them to explain their meanings and relevance when you meet for the interview. Being company certified may mean the manager gave the candidate a gold star! It can also mean an achievement such as an MCSE, Microsoft Certified System Engineer, which is a meaningful and legitimate designation. Many associations offer certifications for various skill levels and knowledge achievement, some of which are meaningful only to the members themselves.

Don't be fooled by fancy or impressive claims, and don't assume that they are bogus. All claims offer interview opportunities.

A note of caution:

In Chapter 1, we identified the potential hiring trap of seeking candidates "in your own image." Be careful that you do not become unduly excited about a candidate whose resume shows parallel experiences to yours. Just because candidates:

- Come from *your* hometown
- Served in the same branch of the service as *you*
- Graduated from the same high school or college as *you*
- Worked for a company or in an industry where *you* have had past experience

These coincidences do *not* ensure that candidates are clones of *you* and deserve to be hired because they will serve the organization as well as you have. (Neither does this indicate they are undeserving of being hired; be sure to keep your perspective here.) Do not fall in love with *yourself* in reviewing a resume!

Step Two: Circle Information That Needs Verification. Circle in red pen claims, dates, and data that require verification. These may include employment dates or alleged facts or figures concerning achievements.

Review employment history claims carefully. Focus on information concerning the months of initial hire or separation from an organization. Candidates stating they worked for ABC Company from 1999 to 2000 may be hiding factual information. This may reflect two years of service (from January 1999 to December 2000), or two weeks of service (from December 1999 to January 2000)!

Statements of achievement must be clarified in quantifiable terms. The hiring trap of rating individual strengths dispro-portionately is often fueled by not verifying claims. You *want* the candidate to have reduced operating expenses by 50 per-cent; you *want* the candidate to have increased revenues by 100 percent; and it is easy to take such statements at face value. Dig deep enough to discover the true meaning.

Circle areas where you need specific clarification of the in-formation. The trap of periscope-depth (or shallow) ques-tioning is evident when you fail to pursue clarification. For example,

- A statement claiming to increase sales 100 percent could mean, "I sold $1.00 of product in a brand-new territory."
- Someone claiming to have hired and trained all new employees in the accounting department could be more accurate by stating, "We hired one new em-ployee in three years and I showed that person where to find the lunchroom."

Usually when candidates list significant legitimate, positive achievements on their resumes, they probably also include the appropriate supporting information. Their claims may read:

- Increased sales by 100 percent, from five million to ten million dollars in one fiscal year
- Hired and trained thirty-five new employees in thirty-six months

The more specific the information the candidates provide, the more likely it is to be legitimate. Generalized statements more frequently prove problematic.

If achievements aren't clearly identified, it is usually an indicator that further probing is necessary. Lack of specifics may indicate a candidate's attempt to use smoke and mirrors. Even when this information is included, seek other forms of verification. A compelling question to ask yourself (and the candidate) is: "How can this information be corroborated?"

People are taught to use action verbs in creating their resumes, but you must look beyond creative language and seek truthful and accurate detailed information. Candidates want to tell you about their responsibilities; you want to learn about their results.

It is critical that you seek additional information on a candidate's claims of having made a significant impact on

- Dollars—increased profit or cost reductions
- Time—reductions in process or turnaround times
- Quality—process or product improvement

These issues are important and achievements in these areas, if verified, can indicate a valuable candidate. These are also areas that readily lend themselves to resume distortion. If a resume contains embellishments, they are probably contained in statements about dollars, time, quality, and earnings. Some candidates believe claims can be made with impunity because many interviewers don't seek verification.

Circle statements of earnings, and be wary if earnings are not listed (especially if you requested them). It is important that you determine a candidate's true current and past earnings. Everyone wants to earn more, and your opportunity may indeed offer a sizeable increase in compensation; however, you need to know the true facts and figures. You do not want to pay $50,000 for a $30,000 employee! You should verify all claims of increased compensation, especially those reflecting sudden jumps in earnings. It is also important that you determine how much of a candidate's compensation has been salaried as opposed to bonus- or performance-based initiatives. High salaries may indicate comfort. High incentive-based earnings may indicate achievement.

Step Three: Circle Information That Needs Clarification. Circle in blue terms or statements that need further explanation. A candidate may be using company jargon or industry-specific terms that imply greater responsibility or achievement than is true. Do not accept statements you do not understand. If you choose to interview the candidate, it is appropriate to seek explanations or definitions; you should request that details be put in layman's or outsider's terms. Never be too embarrassed to admit you do not understand something. Some information distorters are counting on your embarrassment!

- If a candidate claims she is or was a manager, did she manage people? Products? Projects? Information? Geography? Things?
- If a candidate claims he is or was an operations assistant, what does that mean? What operations did he assist? What is his definition of assisting? What were his specific responsibilities?

Keep in mind that organizations can define common workplace terms in different ways. What means one thing in your organization may mean something entirely different to an outsider, and vice versa. When in doubt, seek clarification.

Listed below are forty-nine verbs typically used in resume writing that must be defined precisely.

Analyzed	Eliminated	Interfaced with	Procured
Arranged	Engineered	Introduced	Promoted
Controlled	Established	Investigated	Reduced
Converted	Expanded	Launched	Researched
Coordinated	Forecasted	Led	Saved
Created	Generated	Modernized	Secured
Cut	Implemented	Negotiated	Set up
Designed	Improved	Optimized	Sparked
Developed	Increased	Organized	Systematized
Directed	Initiated	Originated	Trained
Discovered	Installed	Prevented	Triggered
Disseminated	Instituted	Prioritized	Verified
Doubled			

The more blue circles on the reviewed resume, the higher the possibility the candidate has received a degree in embellishment or creative writing!

Step Four: Evaluate the Results of Your Color-Coding. Yellow is good! The greater the number of highlights, the greater the possibility you have an exceptional candidate. Red indicates the need for further verification. Blue indicates the need for further clarification and for definitions. The more red and blue marks you have, the greater your need to probe and look beyond the obvious!

Step Five: Ask Probing Questions. Always rely on your own intellect and managerial experience by asking yourself these three compelling questions:

1. Does the candidate's employment history make sense? (It's not whether you would make the same decisions,

but whether the decisions that were made appear to be reasonable and reflect some level of thoughtful planning. Was the candidate on a consistent path of achievement and then decided to drop out and go live on an island in the Pacific to study native plant life for a couple of years? If so, what does that mean? Is it a negative or a positive?)

2. Are the candidate's job history, education, and achievements *too* perfect? (There is no such thing as a perfect candidate.) The illusion of perfection may indicate a candidate who is aware of a significant weakness and is making a great effort to present himself as someone he's not! Of course, it could also reflect an excellent candidate who knows how to write a good resume! Develop a healthy skepticism about perfection and be open to a possible gift from God!

3. Are the candidate's claimed earning levels reasonable? (You have a basic knowledge of compensation rates, both within your organization and throughout your industry.) Does the candidate claim to have been paid at twice the going rate? To have received salary increases of 50 percent each year? Is the candidate hesitant to show you proof of earnings? Logic and common sense go a long way here.

The Proper Use of Phone Screening

When you have reviewed candidates' resumes and have identified those you believe are worth your consideration for employment, conduct an initial condensed interview or screening over the telephone. If you are not quite sure about candidates, it never hurts to talk with them. It is like chicken soup: What have you got to lose? This strategy has various advantages, including

1. It is an efficient use of your time. Spending an initial fifteen to twenty minutes on the telephone with a candidate may save you from squandering valuable time on an ill-advised formal interview. Some form of contact with the candidate is helpful so that you can be sure you want to invest the time in a personal meeting. Phone screens are also helpful if you cannot schedule an interview on a timely basis (if you are traveling, or if the demands of your current responsibilities make it difficult for you to be immediately available for a formal interview). A phone screen allows you to address candidates quickly, impresses them with your interest and willingness to talk with them, and buys you time.

2. Effective phone screens can become an important part of your decisionmaking. Candidates may look good on paper; however, in a short conversation you may determine there is not a match. The candidates, too, may determine they have no interest in your opportunity, and the phone screen eliminates additional wasted time. Possibly your interest in a candidate will skyrocket because of additional information you gain during a phone conversation.

3. Well-conducted phone screens are more casual and generally more relaxed than a face-to-face interview. Candidates are more comfortable and forthcoming with information than they would be if they were meeting with you formally. The rapport you establish

during the phone screen carries over and will make the formal interview more productive.

4. You have the opportunity to assess candidates' abilities to communicate (at least by way of the telephone). Today, most jobs require some level of phone communication skills, and you can also determine their ability to think on their feet. Although you cannot observe candidates' nonverbal communication, a short phone conversation can yield a wealth of communication indicators.

5. Phone screens also help to eliminate, or at least reduce, subconscious discriminatory factors. In Chapter 1, we discussed the traps of making egg-timer decisions and hiring in your own image. Some potential, unintentional, subconscious negative factors—such as age or physical appearance—that might cause you to fall into these traps can be reduced or neutralized when you screen first by phone. You begin to form an opinion about candidates before you see them.

A Note of Caution

Always consider the potential impact of poor telephone technology. If either you or the candidate is on a cell phone, for example, you run the risk that poor technology will create negative impressions *in both directions*. Being at the mercy of cell technology or conducting the phone screen while driving or sitting in a public place will diminish the quality of the discussion. Conduct phone screens from a permanent landline phone and encourage the candidate to do so as well. Avoid speaker phones if possible.

The Six-Step Phone-Screening Process

The following is a guideline for conducting effective phone screens. Used properly, it will help you in your decisionmaking and establish a preinterview foundation for high-quality succeeding discussions.

Step 1: Initial Contact. By phone or e-mail, contact the candidate to establish a time to conduct a fifteen- to twenty-minute preliminary interview. Typically, you would offer a choice of two times and ask the candidates to confirm the time slots they prefer. If you offer these times, it is imperative that you be available for their choices. Even if you reach them directly, it is best to set a follow-up time for the interview. Both of you need time to prepare. Do not put yourself in the position of having to do an off-the-cuff interview, and nothing can be gained by catching candidates off guard. Giving them a surprise doesn't necessarily work in your favor.

Explain what you want to accomplish; for example, a twenty-minute phone call to ask preliminary questions, address questions they have for you, and determine whether a formal interview is beneficial to both. It is important that you convey enthusiasm and establish the professional manner in which the interviewing process will be handled.

Reconfirm the scheduled time for the interview and agree on who will place the call. If this is unclear, both of you could be staring at your phones, waiting for them to ring!

Step 2: Begin the Phone Screening by Establishing Rapport. Show high interest in the candidates; the best way to do that is by being complimentary. Convey the message that you welcome the opportunity to talk with people of their caliber and explain the objectives of the phone interview.

Your goal is to gather information, respond to the questions they may have, and provide the information that is appropriate at this time. Establish that both you and the candidate will provide more detailed information during the face-to-face formal interview, and that this phone conversation will allow you to get to know each other a little better before you meet. Identify the probable time frame for conducting a formal interview (within one week, three weeks, one month), and ask the candidates whether that timing is convenient and acceptable. If they need to move sooner, you want to be aware of that as early as possible so that you have the choice of expediting your process.

Step 3: Address the Resume's Red and Blue Items. If you probe *three* areas of each, you should be able to determine whether you have a legitimate candidate, and whether you have an interest in moving forward.

You can begin your probing by saying:

"I would like some further clarification on these dates."
"I want to gain a better understanding of your statement.". . .

If candidates are not what they represent themselves to be, you will probably flush this out quickly. A good strategy is to inform candidates at this time of your policy to conduct extensive reference and background checks. If they are uncomfortable with some of their answers, they may choose to restate them or clarify their responses after they hear your statement.

To clarify areas of contention or doubt, you should request that candidates provide specific documentation that can corroborate the claims made on their resumes or in the interviews. Most candidates have access to past performance appraisals, company newsletters, statements of awards, W-2 forms, and so forth. You are within your rights to ask for documentation or corroboration. If documentation is not available, the claims are not automatically guaranteed fraudulent; however, lack of documentation may be cause for concern.

Step Four: Prepare to Answer Typical, Predictable Questions. Most candidates tend to ask the same repetitive questions. You can prepare for them in advance. These questions typically include overviews of the position, the career path—especially anticipated promotional growth—and perhaps an inquiry about compensation. Answer the questions to your level of comfort. Do not appear evasive, but use time as a tool; choose to discuss some of the more detailed inquiries during the formal interview. It is best to delay compensation questions until that time; however, if the candidate's earnings or salary demands are out of your range, discover this early. If compensation is going to be a knockout factor, find this out before you invest significant time in the interview process.

Questions concerning benefits, hiring incentives, and so forth are probably best deferred until you can meet face-to-face. You do not want to be maneuvered into making commitments (or even appearing to do so) you may be unwilling to fulfill later.

Step 5: Decide Whether to Move Forward. If the phone screens result in your deciding not to pursue certain candidates, be sure to let them down gently. You can say that you are interviewing multiple candidates, and are fortunate to have been contacted by some high-caliber and competent professionals. Emphasize that the competition for the position is fierce. You can inform candidates that you don't think there is a good fit or you can say that you will call them within a few days if you want a formal interview. Then follow up with an e-mail or a letter thanking them for their time. State that you have chosen another candidate or that you have narrowed the candidates to a select few, and the candidate, unfortunately, is not among them. Treat unsuccessful candidates with great respect; situations change and you may be willing to consider them for another position in the future. Unsuccessful candidates who have been treated well are more likely to refer their friends and associates who may have different qualifications or a keen interest in pursuing your organization.

For the candidates you decide to pursue further, establish a time for the formal interview and give them three reasons it is in their best interest to talk with you further. This information is solely intended to entice them further and should be targeted toward their personal growth and development. Your comments may include

"The position we have available looks as if it will be a great next step for you in your career growth. It will position you to pursue greater opportunities, either within our organization or on the outside in the future. You can obviously make a valuable contribution to us, but I think we, as an organization, can make a valuable contribution to you and your career."

The reason for encouraging selected candidates is simple: They are probably talking to other organizations and you must impress them with your potential opportunity. You want them to delay accepting pending job offers at least until they have talked with you. You must give them a good enough reason to wait! Many high-quality candidates seem to lose interest or disappear between the phone screen and the first interview. You are responsible for doing an effective job of making candidates realize that you and your organization are worth serious consideration. In the past, candidates were ecstatic just to be granted an interview. Today, the roles have shifted. You are competing for them.

Step 6: Follow Up with an E-Mail or Phone Message. To confirm the next step, tell the candidates that you enjoyed talking with them and that you are looking forward to your meeting face-to-face. Reemphasize that you are committing the time specifically for this interview and that you are making adjustments, changing commitments, or rescheduling other meetings to be available. Raising the candidates' awareness that this is an important commitment for you encourages them to place even more importance on the interview. If they change their minds, they are more likely to cancel rather than ignore the appointments. Candidates will be much more committed when they realize the importance you attach to the interview. People tend to value what has great emphasis placed on it.

Now we will look at interviewing logistics and planning issues.

Interview Logistics

You should consider various factors when preparing for and planning the formal interview. First, be anticipatory; using these factors to your greatest advantage will maximize your results.

The Physical Environment

Your goal is to put candidates at ease and to create an environment that will make them feel comfortable about being open and honest in their responses. The physical environment can have a significant effect on candidates' candor and comfort.

As a general rule, do not interview someone formally across a desk or conference table. Position yourself so that you are on the same level and equal to each other: chairs positioned facing each other in a conversational setting or both of you on the same side of the conference table.

The interview must always be conducted in private and be free of interference. Hold all phone calls. Do not allow interruptions from others. If possible, remove potential distractions. If your office is located on the factory floor where it is noisy, go to a quieter place.

A neutral, nonthreatening location is usually best for initial or early interviews. Impressive offices with visual signs of authority and power can be intimidating.

Review the Resume Again

Review candidates' resumes and your notes from the phone screens for at least fifteen minutes before the interviews. Take the time and effort to refamiliarize yourself with their background information, and review the primary questions you are going to ask. Being unprepared gives the appearance of confusion or of disinterest in them. Questions such as "Are you the candidate who worked for ABC Company or are you the one from XYZ?" do not give the candidate a good impression of your competency or preparedness.

Establish an Environment of Open Communication

Stress the importance of the visit and your appreciation of their dedicating the time to talk with you. As in the phone screen, compliment their experience, education, and qualifications. Tell candidates that you would rather have an interactive conversation and not an interrogation. Interviews by their very nature are stressful for both parties. Do everything you possibly can to build rapport and to allay candidates' stress.

Visibly displaying your listening is also important. Candidates will be more forthcoming and provide a greater volume of in-depth information if they believe you are listening intently and have a genuine interest. Maintain open and attentive body language and use appropriate verbal and nonverbal responses to the candidates' statements. We all feel most comfortable with people who listen and who agree with us. Display that behavior to the candidates you interview.

Interview Length

An interview should not exceed one hour. You and the candidates will probably become less attentive if you continue beyond sixty minutes without a break. If you are engaged in a prolonged interview, take a short fifteen-minute break to refresh and regroup. Allow candidates some privacy and the opportunity to make phone calls, and take some time for yourself as well. It has been estimated that the average American has an attention span of two thirty-minute television shows! After you have been concentrating and communicating for sixty minutes, you serve everyone's best interest by taking a break. If you schedule a candidate for multiple interviews with different people, limit these to one hour each with appropriate break times in between.

If you are interviewing multiple candidates in a back-to-back schedule, take the time between each interview to refresh and review the information for the next candidate. You need to maintain your sharpness. The best candidates may be scheduled toward the end of your interviewing efforts and you do not want to be comatose when they appear.

How Many Interviews?

Never get married on the first date!

You need to conduct multiple interviews with a candidate before you can make an educated hiring decision. Depending on the position, it may be appropriate to schedule five or more meetings. John Korzec said that at Otis, from three to seven or eight interviews are conducted with a successful candidate.

Failing to conduct multiple interviews forces you to make impulsive hiring decisions; it also sends a message to the candidate either that you are desperate or that you have little interest in the quality of candidates you hire. From the candidates' perspective, a job you can land after only one or two interviews can't be very meaningful. Hiring too soon is dumb; why send dumb messages to potential employees?

Multiple Interviewers

Whenever possible, involve others in the interviewing process. If human resources professionals conduct initial interviews before referring candidates to you, they can provide valuable insight and multiple opinions. You can also involve others, including your peers, your managers, your boss, and even key members of the department or team. Because your employees will be affected by the new people you hire, it is usually an excellent strategy to involve your current people in the interviewing process. Although you will make the final decision, their input is helpful. Always remember that those formally involved in the interviewing process must receive appropriate training. When allowing others to participate in choosing the people they will be working with, do not take the risk that someone may ask an inappropriate question or discourage a candidate because of poor interviewing skills. Everyone involved must be trained.

If you have lingering concerns about a candidate, ask others to address them when they do the interviewing. You may also choose to remain silent and see whether other interviewers develop the same concerns. The same advice applies for compelling strengths. Rather than influencing others' perceptions by sharing your assessments before they conduct the interview, address them in a postinterview debriefing. Allow others to form their opinions uninfluenced by your perceptions.

Vary the Interview Locations

If possible, conduct your subsequent interviews in different settings. If the first interview is in the conference room, take candidates to your office for the second, or vice versa. If you have conducted two interviews in your office or facility, consider a third interview off-site; meet for coffee or a meal (provided you can find a private setting where the interview will not be conducted within the earshot of others). Viewing candidates in different environmental settings can be enlightening.

One CEO shared this interesting example:

> We were searching for a candidate to be our vice president of finance. Obviously, this was an extremely important position within our organization, and our decision was being made very carefully. We did a nationwide search, identified five possible candidates, and conducted extensive, in-depth interviews with each of them. The decision on the final candidate was based not only on my perceptions and background checking, but the input of others, including our vice president of human resources and the chairman of our board of directors. The final candidate traveled from a distant city, and after the last interview, I asked him

to extend his visit an extra day. I wanted him to join my wife and I for dinner. I wanted to spend some informal time with the candidate, and valuing my wife's opinion, I wanted her to meet him. Although we had not made a formal job offer, the candidate was very excited, obviously realizing the meaning of the invitation and request to stay over. The dinner that evening proved to be very interesting. When our food was delivered from the kitchen, the candidate was unhappy and became irate. He sent his food back to the kitchen and demanded to see the restaurant manager and the chef. When they approached our table, he berated both of them loudly in front of all of the patrons of the restaurant. My wife and I were both embarrassed by his behavior. He basically talked himself out of a job with his performance at dinner. I believe he was probably attempting to impress us with his high standards. In his mind he was demonstrating that he would not accept less than excellent performance, not only from the people who served him, but also by implication, the people he managed. While I had no problem with his returning food to the kitchen that was not acceptable, I did have a major concern over the way he handled the situation. If he was trying to impress us, his behavior accomplished just the opposite. While witnessing his tirade, I could only envision him doing the same thing to the employees in our office. I would not subject the people in our office to that type of abuse. We finished our meal in relative quiet, and the next morning I thanked him for his time and told him that we had decided not to extend him an offer. When he asked why, I referenced his behavior at dinner, and he was amazed, bordering on insulted, that my standards were not as high as his. He defended his behavior and indicated he was glad that he discovered my shortcomings because he would not want to work for a C.E.O. that was willing to accept less than perfection. I don't believe the man ever truly understood the actual problem!

Although it is not always appropriate to treat your candidates to dinner, it may be enlightening to view their behavior under different circumstances. It could be an eye-opener!

Tours and Walk-Arounds

In most organizations, employment candidates are offered the opportunity to view the work area, walk around the office, and meet key people. Rather than conducting these tours or walk-arounds yourself, consider inviting someone else in your department, group, or on your team to serve as the guide. Select people who would be peers of the candidate. After they have shown the candidate around, ask them in general terms about their perceptions. Although you are not asking them to breach confidentiality or to become informants, you are asking for their general impressions. In the presence of potential peers, candidates may let their guard down and make statements or ask questions they were reluctant to address with you. If the tour guides consider these questions and statements inappropriate or do not believe the candidates would make a welcome addition to the company or culture, they may send you a clear signal. If so, ask them to be as specific as possible in explaining why they were summarily unimpressed. Their impressions could be insightful.

In Chapter 5, we will look at the second phase in your quest to find, hire, and keep peak-performing employees. This is where you are deciding whether you want to invest in *buying* their services.

Planning Assessment Exercise	**Yes**	**No**
1. Do I have a system for evaluating resumes?	___	___

2. Do I effectively address vague or "red flag" statements contained in the resumes of candidates? ___ ___

3. Do I effectively use phone screens as part of my interviewing process? ___ ___

4. Do I plan the physical environment when I interview? ___ ___

5. Do I establish an environment of open communication? ___ ___

6. Do I always conduct multiple interviews with the candidates I hire? ___ ___

7. Do I seek the input of others about the candidates I hire? ___ ___

No responses are opportunities for growth and development.

PART TWO

Hiring Peak Performers

5

Effective Interviewing Skills

Becoming a skilled interviewer is *not* easy. The skills of interviewing are difficult to learn and must be practiced to maintain proficiency. For most, they are not instinctive skills; indeed, they run counter to many of the things we have learned in dealing and communicating with people. The goal of interviewing is to encourage people to open up to you and talk candidly. Many of us have been taught throughout our lives not to pry, not to ask questions about people's backgrounds, not to get personal, and so forth; however, that's exactly what you must do to be an effective interviewer. You must learn to structure your statements and questions in such a way that they invite and encourage people to give you in-depth responses. Most of us learned early in life to structure our communication to elicit quick, short, and to-the-point answers. Consider this conversation:

"How was your day?"—"Fine."
"Anything new?"—"No."
"Are you hungry?"—"Yes."
"What would you like for dinner?"—"What have you got?"

Lack of skill in structuring effective interview questions often causes frontline managers to fall into the trap of talking too much. Ineffective questions lead to short, uninformative responses, and awkward silences set in; these are similar to the so-called dead air in radio broadcasts. When silences occur, managers may blunder in to fill them; but in their attempts to pick up the pace of the interview, they only succeed in dominating the conversation.

In our culture, the ability to encourage people to be open in their communications is a highly valued skill. Professionals in the entertainment and journalism world earn respect, good compensation, and recognition because they demonstrate the rare ability to encourage others to share important information. In many cases, they are seeking a revealing disclosure or the divulging of private, sensational information. You are not seeking sensationalism; all you want is to have people give you honest and accurate information so that you can make an informed hiring decision. Sometimes the interviewing situation is adversarial. The lines are drawn, one person trying to get the other to say something wrong or inappropriate that can be used against them. Many people interviewed for jobs feel that way. They must guard themselves against saying something that could be used as the basis for denying them employment. Your role is to find reasons for hiring them, not to judge them harshly or negatively.

Being an effective interviewer and being an effective investigator have many similarities. The goal of an investigation is to discover the truth. Isn't that also the intent in your interviews? You want to discover the candidates' skills, identify their potential, and predict their future performance.

Do not expect yourself to possess interviewing skills instinctively; that is unrealistic. Do not become overconfident and "shoot from the hip" in designing the structure of your questions or comments. The good news is that these skills can be learned; the question is, are you willing to commit yourself to learning them?

Every interview has two distinct phases, and your role is different in each phase; you must change your communication strategies as the situation demands.

- The *buying* phase—You lead the discussion through the effective use of questions; you evaluate candidates' responses, and determine whether you want to *buy* their services for your organization. You are going shopping!

- The *selling* phase—When you have decided to continue consideration of candidates for employment, you must create excitement in them. You must instill in candidates the desire to learn more about your organization and the opportunity you have available for them. It boils down to making them *want* to come to work for you.

In this chapter we will address the first phase of the interview.

The Buying Phase

Whether it is a first interview or a follow-up interview, there will always be a buying phase during which you will assess candidates' suitability for hire. In later-stage interviews, you may probe specific issues, perhaps even provide candidates with preemployment testing or scenarios that enable you to evaluate their responses. In the first interviews, the buying phase should last a minimum of thirty minutes. As we discussed in Chapter 4, an effective interview should last sixty minutes; initially, you should invest at least half that time evaluating candidates. To avoid egg-timer decisions, be willing to assess candidates' responses and interview style for an extended time, otherwise you may fall prey to knee-jerk reactions: quick decisions based on appearance, hunch, or first impression. You owe it to yourself and to the candidates to be more thorough.

The buying phase is composed of two important stages: beginning the interview and discovering information.

Opening the Interview

The first segment, although of short duration, is important in determining the success of an interview. An effective opening accomplishes two important things:

- It gives candidates a positive first impression of you and the organization.
- It puts candidates at ease initially, setting the stage for open, honest, frank discussion.

The Initial Greeting. If possible, meet candidates in the lobby and walk them to the interview; this allows you to introduce yourself and engage in casual conversation as you walk together, and the candidates will feel more comfortable. Meeting candidates and escorting them eliminates the potentially awkward situation of a formal introduction, taking your seats, and immediately beginning the interview.

If someone else escorts candidates to the interview, stand immediately, greet them as close to the door as possible, warmly introduce yourself, and offer them a seat. Address their comfort; have water, coffee, or soft drinks available, and help candidates feel as welcome as possible. This is *not* the time to attempt to impress candidates with your power and authority. Do not

- Use hand gestures to wave candidates into a seat while you continue a phone conversation.
- Fail to make eye contact or ignore them as they enter, appearing to be focused on their resumes or other reading material.
- Leave them standing awkwardly while you appear to be preoccupied elsewhere.
- Make them wait and cool their heels while you attend to more important tasks.

Honor your appointment schedule. Their time is just as valuable to them as yours is to you. Making candidates wait is disrespectful and rude.

Setting the Stage. Thank candidates for their time; tell them how much you enjoyed reviewing their resumes, talking with them on the phone, and how much you appreciate their willingness to invest their time in talking with you. Be complimentary. This begins to build rapport and may bolster the candidates' confidence.

Establish Expectations. Candidates must know what to expect in the interviewing process.

If there is a possibility that candidates will be interviewing with others, either later the same day or at a future time, they need to know who will conduct the additional interviews and when they will occur. If you require preemployment skill testing or other such activities, candidates need to be aware of these requirements at the beginning of the process. Summarize for them how long you expect to take in making your final decision and extending a job offer. The key here is no surprises for the candidate.

Lower the candidates' initial expectations of time. Tell them that the initial interview will be fairly short and that you will spend more in-depth time together as you proceed through the process. This establishes the expectation of a relatively short interview. This expectation increases your options. If you determine during the initial buying phase that you do not have an interest in certain candidates and you do not wish to *buy* their abilities and services, you have the option of cutting the interview short. You can end the session by explaining that if you desire further interviews, you will contact them within the week to discuss the next step. Candidates will be neither surprised nor offended by the abbreviated interview because it was in line with the initially established expectation.

If you do have an interest in certain candidates and you choose to enter the selling phase, they will hardly be offended when you appear to be giving them more time than you intended; this is a positive sign that the interview is going well and that you have a high interest in talking with them further because you are extending past the time that was initially implied.

Make an Opening Statement. Make a statement informing candidates how the interview will be conducted and what you expect from them. One experienced frontline manager offered this example of her opening statement:

> I know that many interviews can be very stressful. I would much rather we had a conversation as opposed to an interrogation. Do

whatever you need to make yourself comfortable and if you need a break or refreshments, please let me know. I want to learn as much about your background as I can and then I will be happy to tell you about us and answer any questions. I will be taking notes as we talk so please do not let that distract you, and do not attempt to read anything into whether I write something down or not. Many times random thoughts just pop into my mind. If you are ready, I would like to begin by asking . . .

Follow the 80/20 Rule of Interviewing.   This is the key to overcoming the talking-too-much trap. During the buying phase, you will do 80 percent of the *listening* and 20 percent of the *talking*. Unfortunately, many frontline managers do 90 percent of the talking in the initial stages of the interview; this gives candidates opportunities only to grunt or nod in agreement. Your role changes dramatically in the second, or selling, phase however. In the initial stage of the interview, your role is to ask effective questions, then shut up and listen. You cannot make high-quality interviewing decisions if you are not gathering high-quality information from your candidates. You do not gather information when you are talking!

Discovering Information

You must probe to discover the information you think is relevant, not just the information candidates want you to hear. Your goal is to hear "their side of the story"; this requires you to design inquiries that target critical areas for discussion and encourage candidates to provide accurate, relevant information freely and openly. The three most important tools available to you are

- Your real-world needs assessment (discussed in Chapter 2)
- Candidates' resumes (discussed in Chapter 4)
- Your intellect and managerial experience

Used effectively, these tools target the areas you need to explore; then you can decide whether to proceed with a candidate. As we consider various question design options, you should follow four important guidelines:

First, avoid jargon and acronyms. Many words and phrases commonly used in your organization may be meaningless, confusing, or intimidating to candidates. Most candidates will be reluctant to admit they do not understand your statements and references for fear of appearing dumb or of being embarrassed. Their responses may be distorted and, at best, the use of confusing terms will slow down the interview. Using jargon also shows insensitivity to candidates.

Second, avoid using leading questions. Telegraphing the obvious answer usually produces invalid responses. Asking, "Did you consider all the risks before you made your decision?" leads candidates to respond with the answer they think you want to hear. An appropriate rewording would be, "What risks did you consider before making your decision?"

Third, questions can be used to maintain control of the interview. If candidates ramble in answering a question, you can make a redirecting statement and transition into another question. "Excuse me, in deference to our time, I should like to move on. Let me ask you this . . . "

If candidates appear to duck a question or deviate from answering what you asked, you can use this technique: "Perhaps I wasn't clear in presenting my question. Let me phrase it differently. How would you . . . ?"

Controlling the interview is important; however, never prevent candidates from elaborating or providing additional appropriate information. As long as their responses are relevant and on topic, give them plenty of freedom in answering your inquiries.

Finally, remember that the interview questions you design are intended to answer four relatively simple inquiries:

1. Are candidates able to demonstrate *specific* examples of having performed identical or similar tasks to those they will be required to perform in the position you have available?

2. Are candidates able to give specific examples of when they demonstrated the behaviors necessary to work within your organization's culture, policies, and boundaries? Are they able to convince you that they do not indulge in disruptive behaviors that will hinder their performance and the performance of those around them?

3. Do candidates offer specific reasons to indicate that they can be trained to accomplish the necessary tasks within your organization's capability to provide training and development?

4. Are candidates an upgrade to the position and will they make a positive contribution to the organization?

To satisfactorily answer these four issues, you can use various question design options to discover the appropriate information. These fall into two groups: traditional interview questions and situationally targeted questions.

Traditional Interview Questions. These are the primary types of questions used generally throughout the interviewing process. Some may be more comfortable for you than others, but all are effective when used appropriately. Never use only one type or style of question. It is important to vary your questioning technique and pattern to uncover accurate and honest information. Rarely does one specific question elicit the complete package of information you are seeking. Typically, interview questions are linked together in a cascade, or cluster, configuration. One question may be used to set up another; in many cases, a topic may have to be revisited with differently structured questions to gather all the necessary information.

Here are seven effective traditional interview questions:

Icebreakers. Simple questions, easily answered honestly with no perceived threat. They are used exclusively at the beginning of all interviews in a series of two or three quick inquiries designed to help the interviewee feel comfortable in providing candid answers.

"Did you have a long drive to get here?"
"Was traffic exceptionally bad?"
"Do you have much of a ride when you leave here?"

Closed-Ended Questions. Inquiries intended to elicit a short one- or two-word response, usually yes, no, or a specific piece of information. They set up other questions, and they are usually the first question in a cluster. Closed-ended questions encourage candidates to take a specific position on an issue; from here, you can begin an in-depth discussion. Closed-ended questions are also valuable in confirming specific information.

"Have you held more than one position with your current
    employer?"

(Appropriate yes or no response.)

Chicago Public Library
Harold Washington Library Center

Customer ID: ********0482

Items that you checked out

Title:
 Ask the right questions, hire the best
 people /
ID: R0412580298
Due: Friday, January 29, 2016

Title:
 Hiring : how to find and keep the
 best people /
ID: R0170064164
Due: Friday, January 29, 2016

Title:
 Finding, hiring, and keeping peak
 performers : every manager's
 guide /
ID: R0176331797
Due: Friday, January 29, 2016

Total items: 3
Account balance: $0.00
Friday, January 08, 2016 5:10 PM
Checked out: 5
Overdue: 0

Please retain for your records.
Thank you for using CPL's self
        service.

"What are the total sales in your territory to date?"

(Appropriate response is a specific dollar amount.)

"Are you open to relocation or do you prefer to stay in this area?"

(Appropriate response is a choice of either/or.)

Open-Ended Questions. Inquiries intended to elicit a *wordy* or lengthy response. Used to seek expanded answers, including examples of previous experience behaviors and performance. These questions are used repeatedly throughout the interview. They can be positioned as follow-ups to closed-ended questions to seek further information.

"Have you enjoyed working for EFG, Inc.?"

(Yes)
Open-ended follow-up:

"What have you enjoyed most about your experience at EFG, Inc.?"

Open-ended questions can also be grouped together in their own cluster; it is safe to assume that the more open-ended questions you use, the more effective the interview will be.

Typically, open-ended questions begin with statements such as

"What did you . . . ?" "Explain . . . "
"Describe . . . " "How would you . . . ?"
"In what way . . . ?" "If you could . . . ?"
"Tell me about . . . " "Please cite some examples of. . . "

Restatement/Confirmation.   Repeating back an answer encourages candidates to offer additional information. This type of inquiry invites them to take and defend a firm position. Used effectively to test honesty and self-assurance, these questions are often used following an open-ended inquiry. They can also be used to bring closure to one area of questioning while moving on to another.

Restatement/confirmation inquiries must be stated in the form of a question; they are usually enhanced when you raise your voice inflection at the end of the statement.

"To be sure that I understand, you said your company is
   filing Chapter 11?"
"To avoid any misunderstandings, I thought I heard you say
   you didn't believe poor quality to be a serious issue?"
"Did I hear your statement correctly? You felt you should
   have been given the promotion?"

Strengths and Weaknesses.   Inquiries that invite candidates to share candid assessments of their strengths and weaknesses. Typically used to assess honesty and the ability and willingness to self-assess.

"What are your three primary strengths in the area of
   customer service?"
"What would you say are your three biggest weaknesses?"
"As you balance out your own personal strengths and
   weaknesses, what are the most significant examples of
   both?"

Strength/weakness questions are usually followed with additional requests for examples or assessments of effect.

Tactful Encouragement. A straightforward inquiry designed to ask for more specific information. Usually used immediately after a response and can be effective in encouraging nervous or reluctant candidates to open up. These inquiries usually incorporate a variation of the statement "tell me more about that."

> "That was an interesting response. Tell me more about that."
> "I found that very interesting. What more can you tell me?"
> "You mentioned problems with your previous boss. Can you expand on that?"

Hypothethicals. These questions are usually based on general scenarios and are normally positioned as the first question in a cluster. These inquiries present a hypothetical question or situation and ask for a response. Hypotheticals frequently begin with statements such as "What if . . . ?" and "Just suppose . . . "

> "What if a customer gave you an ultimatum: Either deliver the product within twenty-four hours or cancel the order? What would you do?"
> "If you could change one thing about your current company, what would it be?"
> "If you were given the opportunity to design your perfect job, and money wasn't an issue, what would that job be?"

Situationally Targeted Questions. These inquiries are used in specific situations. Their use is usually dictated by the response to a previous question: If candidates make a statement that seems odd or inconsistent, you would use a situationally targeted question.

> "I am not sure I am in agreement with what was just said.
> Did you see that as a positive outcome? . . . Why?"

When candidates appear to be trying to lead you into an area where they can provide self-serving information, you may choose to begin another line of questioning to change the subject and come back to the topic later from a different direction.

> "We got off the subject a few minutes ago and I would like
> to ask you something more about that. Did you really
> mean . . . ?"

These questions are particularly helpful when "red flags" or areas of potential problems occur during an interview and you want to probe these more extensively. Situationally targeted questions tend to be used as midpoint inquiries in a cluster and are also used extensively in later rounds of interviewing. They are effective for burrowing in to discover in-depth, specific information.

Delayed Response.　These questions revisit information previously discussed. Using a delayed sequence, they are especially effective in verifying facts and confronting inconsistencies. Delayed response inquiries can be used at any time to reopen information discussed at an earlier point. It is never too late to introduce a delayed response.

> "Earlier you mentioned problems with a team member.
> How did you respond to that?"

"In a previous interview, you said you were involved in a new product launch that did not go very well. What were the reasons it failed?"

"I'm intrigued by the circumstances you mentioned earlier concerning your company's merger. What criteria did you use to make the decision to seek another job?"

Negative Probes. These questions are intentionally presented in a negative format. They are intended to position candidates either to support a weak position or to offer a response of disagreement. These probes are typically used to flush out "yes men" or candidates who are "terminal agreers," wanting to support everything that you say. Some people are anxious to agree with everything you say and they are just waiting for you to tell them what they should agree with! The content of these questions may or may not reflect your true perceptions.

"I don't think it's fair to punish employees for being late to work. Don't you agree?"

"We have the highest prices in our industry and pricing is never a problem with our customers. Price is just not a relevant issue. What do you think?"

"If an employee is faced with an unsafe circumstance, I think he should do whatever it takes to get the job done and deal with the safety issue later. I'm sure you agree, don't you?"

Positive Probes. The opposite of negative probes, these inquiries presented in a positive format once again ask candidates to support or to take a contrary position. These inquiries are valuable in encouraging candidates to add supporting information. These questions may or may not reflect your position or true feelings.

"I really believe employees should be willing to start early or work late if necessary to accomplish a special project successfully. Don't you agree? Why?"

"I think strong dress code policies are very important. I'm sure you would agree. Tell me your thoughts."

"We are committed to a lean manufacturing process, which I'm sure you would support. Why do you think that it is important?"

"I think employees should go to the human resource department if they feel they are being treated unfairly. Have you ever taken an action like that? Tell me more about it."

Transition Questions. Combinations of statements and closed-ended questions intended to close one area of discussion and move on to another. They are used effectively when you are confident that you have gathered enough information or you want to divert candidates' attention temporarily by moving to another subject before you return to the current topic. These inquiries are usually positioned to receive a short statement of agreement and are similar to the questions used in controlling the interview.

"With so much for us to talk about, I think it would be better if we moved on to another subject. Is that okay with you?"

"This is really interesting information and I may want to learn more about it later. Right now I would like to discuss [add the topic]. Are you comfortable with that?"

"This discussion makes me think of some other important questions I would like to ask. Can we move on to something else?"

These inquiries position you to move on with the candidate's agreement. To a degree, you are partnering to determine the agenda.

General to Specific Probes.   These general inquiries are structured to encourage a specific response. They are used effectively to determine whether candidates are reluctant to provide information in a certain area. Sequentially delivered, each inquiry increases in "specificity" until an acceptable detailed response is obtained. You offer a general statement or question that encourages candidates to provide specific information. If their responses are general in nature, you ask a slightly more targeted question. If you find it necessary to increase your specificity more than three times on an inquiry, you have probably uncovered an area of concern or discomfort.

Example:

INQUIRY: "Tell me about your previous job with XYZ Information Systems."
RESPONSE: "It was a good experience."
INQUIRY: "What were your specific duties there?"
RESPONSE: "Oh, it was a small company and we all did everything."
INQUIRY: "You must have had a primary responsibility. What was it?"
RESPONSE: "Not really, I just did whatever my manager told me to do."

You could assume three things about this candidate:

1. He is reluctant to discuss his experience with XYZ Information Systems.
2. He really has nothing to say. (The lights are on but nobody's home!)

3. He is a refugee in the federal government's witness protection program.

Aggressive Confrontation. A direct statement of challenge or contention intended to increase pressure on candidates and invite them to defend or explain a questionable answer. Some managers may feel more comfortable with this questioning structure than others; they usually employ it to challenge seemingly inconsistent responses that lack credibility.

"I don't mean to be rude, but that statement made no sense. Can you explain it more clearly?"
"A statement that you reduced costs by 65 percent sounds almost fanciful. Tell me specifically how you did that."
"I find that last statement hard to believe. Is there anything further you can tell me to make me more comfortable with what you have said?"

These inquiries can also yield some indication of how candidates may deal with conflict and criticism. Even if you find aggressive confrontations uncomfortable, be prepared to use these kinds of questions when necessary. Failing to do so may leave important information uncovered. Aggressive confrontation must be presented with respect, and managing your tone of voice and body language are essential. You are an interviewer, *not* a homicide detective. Be careful not to use aggressive confrontations inappropriately.

Specific Cascade. These inquiries are structured to invite candidates to offer a series of specific responses. Usually formatted in a three-two-one delivery, these inquiries can be helpful in getting shy or reserved candidates to open up. They can also be used to ask candidates to consider differing sides of an issue.

"Tell me three reasons you decided to change jobs, two things you want to be sure to avoid with your next employer, and one thing your next job must have to make you happy."

"Tell me three things you really like about your current position, two things you do not enjoy, and one thing that you find absolutely unacceptable."

"Tell me about three significant successes you have had in the last thirty days, two things that didn't go as well as you would have liked, and one thing you would do differently if given another chance."

"What are three things your current manager does well, two things he doesn't do well, and one thing he does that you would never do if you were in his position?"

Subjective Rating.   Three-step inquiries can be formatted to invite a positive or negative response. They are particularly effective in assessing candidates' abilities to look at the other side of the story. The critical factor is how you position steps 2 and 3 to influence the type of response expected. They can provide insight into whether candidates use broad vision and see all sides of an issue, or whether they are narrowly focused. They are particularly effective with candidates who appear to be either extremely negative about a particular subject or extremely positive, even "Pollyanna-ish." These questions include a statement of inquiry, a candidate's response, and steps 2 and 3 as follow-up questions.

Step 1:
INQUIRY: "On a scale of 1 to 10, rate your current manager's leadership ability."
RESPONSE: "I would rate her a 6."

Step 2:
INQUIRY: "Why didn't you rate her *lower?*"

(This question invites candidates to identify *positive* attributes about their current managers. This inquiry is especially effective if you expect a negative or low rating from the candidate.)

Step 3:
INQUIRY: "Why don't you rate her higher? Share with me some of her weaknesses."

Step 1:
INQUIRY: "On a scale of 1 to 10, how would you rate your personal efforts at quality improvement?"
RESPONSE: "Oh, I would rate myself a 7."

Step 2:
INQUIRY: "Why wouldn't you rate that number *higher?*"

(This inquiry invites candidates to identify negative factors. It allows you to assess whether they can look at things objectively.)

Step 3:
INQUIRY: "Why didn't you rate yourself lower? Tell me the things you do well concerning quality improvement."

Situational Role Playing.　Similar to hypotheticals, these inquiries set up a realistic situation and ask candidates to respond. These questions tend to be used more frequently and effectively in later-stage interviews. The situations can be generalized, or they may target circumstances that candidates would encounter if they joined your organization. You can also use situational role playing to describe circumstances that have been poorly handled in the past and to probe for new strategies or alternatives. Presented properly, these inquiries can be valuable opportunities to learn something from the candidate.

"If you had an employee who had a track record of good performance and a series of excellent ratings on his past performance appraisals, but who suddenly became disruptive by showing disrespect in his dealings with his peers, how would you respond to that?"

"If you felt you were being asked to do something unethical or perhaps illegal by someone in authority, how would you handle that?"

"If you learned that one of your peers was taking computer software purchased by the organization home to download onto his personal computer, how would you respond to that circumstance? Would your response be different if he were removing confidential information and storing it elsewhere?"

Assessing Candidates' Responses.   The purpose of your interview questioning efforts is to elicit a response or to gain information from candidates. Questions are only a tool in your discovery. The most important part of the *buying* phase is what you do with the information that surfaces. As we discussed, candidates will always present themselves in their best light. Be committed to probing through their initial self-serving responses to find the real content of their messages.

If you receive the positive answers you want to hear, do *not* accept them at face value. (That is an example of periscope-depth questioning.) Probe deeper to assess the validity of their response.

Vary your questioning technique to avoid channeling or influencing candidates' responses. Asking only positive, "puff ball," easy questions results in candidates' appearing perfect; asking only negative, challenging questions results in their appearing unacceptable. If you pose the question, "When did you stop abusing your family?" it is doubtful that candidates can create *any* responses that would be acceptable.

Egg-timer decisions result in your forming quick, impulsive, subjective opinions or assumptions about candidates; you then ask questions subconsciously structured to support your initial impression. Overcome that trap by using three deep-questioning cascades and by varying your inquiries to allow the candidate to offer a broad-based response. Pursue information that is inconsistent or causes you discomfort.

When so-called red flags appear or areas of concern surface, stay focused on the topic or revisit it. Do not close an interview with open red flags unless you plan to address them in your next session.

It is appropriate to invest five or six questions on a topic to gain the information you need. Relentless probes may be necessary; however, realize that if you probe too aggressively, at some point candidates will see your questioning as badgering. It may be an effective strategy to move into other areas and reintroduce a cluster of delayed-response questions later in the interview or during a follow-up session.

Question Design Strategies to Address Specific Responses

The following is a general guideline for selecting the types of questions to use in specific circumstances. These recommendations are not all inclusive, and if alternative strategies are working well for you, continue to use them.

Circumstance	Question Design
Initial greeting	Ice breakers Open-ended questions
Probing education and experience (highlights on resume assessment)	Closed-ended questions clustered with open-ended Tactful encouragement Specific cascade
Confirming specific information (red circles on resume)	Closed-ended questions clustered with open-ended Restatement/confirmation Strengths/weaknesses
Seeking clarification (blue items on resume assessment)	Closed-ended questions clustered with open-ended Restatement/confirmation Negative probes Positive probes Aggressive confrontation

Responding to Candidate Behaviors

Behavior	Question Design
1. Candidate appears to be enhancing experience, implying greater influence or responsibility in achievements. (Frequently demonstrated with "we" or "I" references to inquiries of clarification.)	*Seek specific clarification* • Closed-ended questions "Were you directly responsible for that?" • Restatement/confirmation "I want to be sure I understand accurately, was that your sole achievement?" • Tactful encouragement "Wow, that's an interesting achievement. Tell me more about it."

(continues)

(continued)

Responding to Candidate Behaviors

Behavior	Question Design
	• Aggressive confrontation "That sounds like an awful lot for one person to accomplish. Did you achieve that solely through your own efforts?" • Specific cascade "Tell me three things you did to accomplish that, two contributions from others that were very helpful, and one thing you learned from that experience." • Subjective rating "On a scale of 1 to 10, one being low, rate the support of involvement of others in that project. Why didn't you rate that lower?"
2. Candidate appears evasive, unwilling or unable to disclose detailed information.	*Seek in-depth information* • Open-ended "What are some of the things you accomplished during that time? Tell me more about that." • Strengths/weaknesses "What three strengths do you have that helped you during that time? What are your weaknesses that hindered your ability to deal with that?" • Tactful encouragement "That sounds challenging. I am sure you can tell me more about that."

(continues)

- Hypotheticals
"What if you were in that same exact situation again, what would you do differently? Tell me about that."
- General to specific probes
"That sounds challenging, was it?" "What was most difficult?" "What is the single most important thing you learned from that?"
- Aggressive confrontation
"I am not getting much information on this, are you reluctant to talk about it? ... Why?"

3. Candidate appears to be well practiced or trained in interviewing skills. "Too perfect."

Vary your technique to avoid predictability of questions and ask thought-provoking opinion inquiries

- Hypotheticals
"What if you were in a decision-making situation and you didn't have the latest information? What would you do? ... How would you do that?"
- Delayed response
"Earlier you talked about how well you handled the problem. What did you do personally to allow the problem to grow in seriousness or intensity?" (Repeatedly use the delayed response.)
- Negative probe
"I don't think your boss was right in handling it that way, do you? ... What would you have done differently?"

(continues)

(continued)

Behavior	Question Design
	• Specific cascade "Tell me about three of your strongest skill areas, two things your current boss would tell me to watch out for in you, and one potential problem we might have in working together." • Situational role-playing "We experience this a lot (describe the situation). What three options would you recommend in dealing with it?"
4. Candidate appears very negative toward current employer.	*Identify source of unhappiness and probe candidate's objectivity* • Restatement/confirmation "Did I hear you say your boss was totally at fault?" • Hypotheticals "From a hypothetical situation, is there anything you could have done differently to avoid the problem?" • Delayed response "Tell me once again why you dislike working there so much." • Positive probe "Oh, I agree; they should have handled it differently. What should they have done?" • Aggressive confrontation "I don't think the policy was all that wrong. What can you tell me to convince me it was?" • Specific cascade "Tell me your manager's

(continues)

three biggest weaknesses, two strengths she has, and one valuable lesson she has helped you learn."

- Subjective rating
  On a scale of 1 to 10, 1 being low, how would you rate your manager's handling of that situation? Why didn't you rate it lower?"

5. Candidate appears to blame others for problems, distancing himself from responsibility

- Open-ended questions
  "Tell me some of the areas you struggle with. . . . Can you give me some examples?"

- Strengths/weaknesses
  "What three strengths would your manager tell me you possess? What weaknesses would he identify?" Tell me about those."

- Hypotheticals
  "Is it ever a possibility that your teammates' strategies could work?"

- Negative probe
  "I agree that decision was terrible. I think it should have been handled differently, don't you? How differently?"

- Aggressive confrontation
  "It seems like everyone else is always at fault. That seems hard to believe. Do you ever make mistakes?"

- Subjective rating
  "On a scale of 1 to 10, 1 being low, how would you rate your handling of the problem? Why didn't you rate it higher?"

6

Interviewing to
Discover Peak Performance

Your role as an interviewer is to predict the future. To do that,
you must possess as much precise and accurate information
and data as possible.

Throughout the next two chapters, you will see a series of
questions designed to help you gather this information and to
evaluate a candidate's relevant past with an eye to seeing the
future. You will not become a psychic . . . merely a mortal with
real-world skill in interviewing. Note that many of the questions are clustered together in sequences and use the various
question designs discussed in Chapter 5. Although every interview offers spontaneous opportunities for specialized questions
and discussion, it is *mandatory* that you preplan the questions.
No two interviews are identical, but you must strive for an
overall consistency. You cannot make decisions on which candidate to hire if you are not comparing similar information. In
looking for specific skills and experience, you must ask every
candidate the same questions concerning those areas. Also,
from a legal point of view, you must be consistent in your
questioning of all candidates. You cannot ask questions of one

candidate that you do not ask of *every* candidate. Preparation enhances consistency.

For each interview that you plan to conduct, print your series of predetermined questions and place them in a notebook. Leave enough space under each question to make notations of the candidate's response, areas of concern, or additional questions on that topic you may want to ask as a result of the discussion. Inform candidates that you will be taking notes during the interview and invite them to do so as well. Be careful that you do not play the role of a court stenographer as opposed to that of effective interviewer. Your notes should be quick summarizations, jotted in your own personal shorthand, and you must always maintain appropriate eye contact with the candidate. Focus your attention on the candidate and briefly address your notes.

Avoid allowing the interview to morph into an interrogation by using an encouraging pattern of speech. Interrogations are rapid-fire patterns of:

Question . . . Answer
Question . . . Answer
Question . . . Answer

An effective interview is patterned:

Question . . . Answer
Comment
Question . . . Answer
Comment
Question . . . Answer
Comment

Your comment can be structured:

"That's really interesting!"
"That's a great example!"
"What a great experience!"

Your comments can be positive utterances:

"Wow!"
"Mmm!"
"Oh?!"

Your comments can be nonverbal affirmations such as raised eyebrows, nodding the head, hand stroking chin.

Use the various forms of encouraging speech patterns to encourage candidates' responses and to avoid intimidating them.

Effective interview questioning follows this guideline:

- Ask candidates whether they possess the skills and experience you are seeking. (They usually say yes!)
- Ask them to cite precise examples of when they have used those skills or to discuss the applicability of their experience. (This is much more difficult, and some candidates cannot give you relevant examples of a claimed skill.)
- Ask additional probing questions to determine the value and depth of their skills and experience (this strategy separates illusion from reality).

Behavioral or experience-based interviewing, extremely popular today, stresses the belief that the best predictor of the future is the past. You can safely assume that what candidates have done in the past they will continue to do in the present and the future. Typically, if you are interviewing a legitimate peak performer who excels in her job, she will continue to do so if she joins your organization. If you have a past poor or mediocre performer, the outcomes will probably be consistent. Does a leopard ever change its spots? Rarely, and only if there is a compelling reason.

Consider this question throughout the interviewing process: "Will it be any different for the candidates here?" If you provide an environment similar to those they have been working in, chances are great that you will receive performances consistent with their pasts. For peak performers, you want to continue to provide the types of incentives, challenges, leadership, and culture in which they thrive. Can you do that? For lesser performers, you have to consider your ability and that of the organization to offer alternatives. If you can do something different to create a better environment, perhaps performance growth will occur. The key is determining what needs to be different and whether you can provide it. Many managers believe that they can take marginal performers and somehow turn them around. Does that ever occur? Occasionally. In reality, most of the times when we embark upon a "reclamation project" with new employees, we crash and burn in a blaze of failure and frustration.

Is it possible for candidates to improve their patterns of performance once they join your organization? Of course—provided they have a proven track record of the willingness and the ability to learn and adapt new procedures. If they consistently blame others for their performance problems and refuse to take personal responsibility for the outcomes, it is just a matter of time until you become the target of blame. Is it possible that candidates can learn from past failure, or even rise above a past termination? Of course; many successful people have failed at or have been fired from previous jobs. The key is determining what they have learned from the experience.

In assessing candidates' past work history, look for trends. One success or failure does not a career make! Do they have trends of promotion? Have their responsibilities increased as their careers developed? Do they show trends of working for "bad bosses"? (Anyone can have a bad boss; a flock of them indicates something else!) Do they exhibit "loser's limp"—lame excuses as to why they have never been completely successful? Learning and growing from adversity can be a powerful experience for many. Unfortunately, too many people are unwilling to make that journey.

Discovering Intrinsic Traits

Along with the areas of assessment identified in Chapter 2, you must evaluate three additional critical intrinsic traits in your candidates. These three traits alone may define the difference between adequate employees and peak performers. If you can accurately determine the level of these attributes in your candidates, your hiring success will be positively influenced.

The Ability and Willingness to Subordinate Self

A huge negative trend appears more prevalent in today's workplace: the perception of personal entitlement. Many people perceive they are *entitled* to agree with everything they are asked to do, and if they don't agree, they should be absolved of responsibility or not held accountable. If the organization is making a change they don't agree with, it's wrong and they shouldn't have to go along with it. If their managers give them tasks they don't agree with, they shouldn't have to perform them. There is also a perception that if employees don't agree with a decision, they are *entitled* to vocalize their disagreement to everyone within earshot. The bottom line is that more people in the workplace today feel they are entitled to be reincarnations of Frank Sinatra and go through life singing *My Way*.

The ability to overcome perceived entitlement and embrace directives from their managers and the overall organization is a valuable trait in employees. A key evaluation question: Do candidates have the ability and willingness to carry out their responsibilities whether they agree with them or not? This is not meant to imply that peak-performing employees willfully follow directives that are immoral, illegal, or unethical. It does address the importance of their dealing appropriately with circumstances, decisions, and strategies they oppose. Do they possess the ability to overcome their opposition and support new policy?

Employees possessing the ability and willingness to subordinate self are willing to contribute their ideas and opinions, yet voice opposition when they consider it appropriate. Once a decision is made to move forward, however, they overcome their personal objections and dedicate themselves to success. They are vocal during planning and supportive during accomplishment.

Employees who do not have this ability may withhold support and position themselves to say, "I told you so." They have a stake in failure—they get to be right. You do *not* need to hire more of those!

Determining whether candidates possess this ability can be difficult. Effective background and reference checks can provide the opportunity to discuss the issue with past employers and peers; always address it if given the opportunity.

Interview Question Suggestions.
> "Give me an example of a circumstance where you have been asked to follow through on a decision when you were not in total agreement."
> "How did you handle that?"
> "What was the ultimate outcome? Tell me more about that."

"Have you ever been in a circumstance where you've been asked to do something you didn't agree with, and if it failed or ran into trouble, you would have been proved right?"

"Was it uncomfortable to be in a position where succeeding meant proving yourself wrong?"

"How did you communicate your disagreement to others and what was the outcome?"

"How would handle that differently in the future?"

Behaviors and Activities Defined by Responsibility, Not by Like

Unfortunately, many employees today resist assignments and tasks if they don't like to do them. Some people redesign their jobs by performing the things they *like* to do very well and simply ignoring the tasks they don't like. These tasks then remain undone or become the responsibility of others; such employees may even procrastinate until a crisis is created. Some employees are vocal when they don't *like* to do something. They communicate to everyone around them that they feel put upon or are being treated unfairly because they have to do something they don't *like* to do.

Real-World Example:

A service manager for a company that manufactured, installed, and provided service for food processing equipment was hiring three new service technicians. One of the job requirements of a technician was to be on call during predetermined nights or weekends. On a rotating basis, service technicians were required to travel on-site and repair equipment breakdowns during nontraditional working hours. This requirement was naturally a source of displeasure for those whose turn it was to provide this service. The service manager said, "When we hire technicians, we explain very clearly that they will be required periodically to carry an emergency beeper and respond if necessary to our customers. Whether it's 3:00 A.M. or in the middle of Sunday dinner, if a customer has problems with our equipment, we have to respond immediately. When we interview candidates, they always say that they are very willing to take their turn in the on-call rotation. However, once hired and it comes down to providing the service, most people complain about it. Reality sets in and we get a lot of griping because they had to leave a family outing or were interrupted during a favorite TV show or football game and were required to work. It's a part of the job, whether we like it or not.

The service manager decided that he needed to find employees who saw being on-call as a positive opportunity to serve customers. He wanted to find people who would look forward to providing this off-hour service. In his quest to find these potential employees, the service manager contacted various professional employment services and a consultant specializing in recruiting. When the service manager described what he was looking for, the consultant replied, "That type of candidate does not exist. Anyone who is sitting around just waiting to be called at odd or inconvenient hours is probably someone you really don't want to hire. The most important thing to concentrate on is finding people who, even though they may not *like* having to provide the service, have the ability to provide it without customers or coworkers knowing of their dislike or unhappiness."

The key to success in this hiring situation was finding candidates who met their responsibilities and were not governed by what they liked to do.

Interview Question Suggestions.
   "Tell me three things that you are required to do but that you really dislike in your current job."
   "Do you ever try to get around having to do them?"

"Do the people you work with or your customers know that you really dislike those tasks?"

"What impact does your dislike of those tasks have on your overall performance?"

"In the past we had an employee who disliked providing a particular service to our customers. When it was necessary for him to do it, he complained loudly, not only to his peers, but, unfortunately, to the customer as well. Have you ever worked with someone like that?"

"Have you ever been in a job situation where you had to do something you didn't want to do?"

"How did you handle it?"

"Why are you able to handle those challenges better than some of the other people in the organization?"

Or you could structure your questions as negative probes:

"I don't think it's fair that employees should be consistently asked to do things they don't want to do. Don't you agree?"

"How should employees react when they are asked to do something they don't want to do?"

"What would you do if you were consistently asked by your boss to do a task you just hated to do?"

"Give me an example of a time when that has happened."

Work Ethic

Predicting a candidate's work ethic is difficult, and for many managers it is perhaps the most critical assessment of all. All candidates interviewing for a job are going to proclaim their possession of an exceptional work ethic; they will tell you,

"Nobody works harder or longer than I do. I do whatever it takes to get the job done."

Probably one of the dumbest interview questions you could ask is, "Do you have a strong work ethic?" If you get a response other than a resounding "Of course," terminate the interview immediately (your candidate is brain dead!); however, that question could be valuable as a setup if followed by an open-ended question such as, "Give me some examples of your work ethic." The problem here is that most candidates have practiced their responses for those types of questions.

You must be creative in your questioning if you are going to address work ethic appropriately.

Interview Question Suggestions.
"How do you define work ethic?"
"Have you ever worked with someone who, in your opinion, had a terrible work ethic?"
"Describe some of the specific behaviors that demonstrated a poor work ethic."
"Have you ever demonstrated any of those behaviors?"
"Have you ever been accused of having a poor work ethic? Tell me about that."
"If I were to ask your manager about your work ethic, what would she say? Why?"
"It is always difficult to balance quality of life issues and work ethic. How do you maintain that balance?"
"Give me three examples of circumstances where work demands have interfered with your personal life, two things you did to address those circumstances, and one thing you have learned from those experiences."

The issue of work ethic should also be addressed during reference and background checks. A great question to ask a former employer is: "On a scale of 1 to 10, 1 being low, how would you rate (the candidate's) work ethic? Why?"

High-Impact Interview Questions

The following are some of the favorite interview questions from the experts who provided information for this book. When asked, "What questions do you find most effective in your efforts to have candidates provide open and honest information," these were their recommendations:

Harry E. Chambers:

> As the author, I would like to share some of my personal favorite interview questions. I think it's important to assess candidates' abilities to deal with challenging and difficult situations. I want to know how they respond when the going gets tough. I pose this question:
>
> > "I'm going to give you three terms and I want you to choose the term that most closely describes you. Gotta win. Hate to lose. Doing the best I can."
>
> There is no right or wrong answer and the important information usually surfaces in the follow-up question. If the candidate's response is "Gotta win," the follow-up question is, "Well, nobody wins all the time; how do you deal with it when you don't win?" If the candidate's response is "Hate to lose," the follow-up question is, "That's interesting, how do you deal with it when you do lose?" If the candidate says, "Doing the best I can," the follow-up question is, "How do you deal with it when your best isn't good enough?"

(The answer I am really looking for is *hates to lose*. I perceive *gotta win* as Pollyana-ish and *doing the best I can* is frequently the rationalization of a failed objective.)

I also like to assess candidates' abilities to look at themselves objectively, and I use this question:

> "If I were to talk candidly with your current manager, what would she tell me are your three biggest strengths? What would she tell me are your three biggest weaknesses?"

Another variation of this question:

> "If I were to ask your manager if there was one improvement she would like to see in you, what would it be? Do you agree? Tell me more."

I also like to probe candidates' competitive natures. All organizations, no matter which sector of the economy they represent, are much more competitive than ever before in our economic history. I prefer using a closed-ended question as a setup to a request for specific examples:

> "Do you consider yourself a competitive person?"
> "What makes you say that?"
> "Can you give me three examples of times when you have reacted favorably to a competitive situation?"

If candidates cite only examples of winning at competitive athletics, I ask them to focus on workplace competition. I am surprised that many candidates cannot respond favorably to these questions beyond a typical "jock" response.

Mike Devereaux, Vice President, Military Division, Lucas Group:

I am extremely interested in finding out how people got where they are. Not so much what they did, but why they did it. I ask a lot of questions like:

> "Tell me why you made that decision. Tell me why you did things that way."
>
> "Tell me why you decided to handle that the way you did."

I want to know the thought process behind their behavior. I also want to know how they deal with adversity.

> "How do you overcome adversity?"
>
> "Tell me about a difficult situation you've been in and how you've dealt with it."
>
> "What specifically have you done to pull yourself up a notch without relying on other people to pull you up?"

I also want to know the things they have done to bring about change. What they've done differently than anyone else.

> "Did you change any operating procedures? Tell me about them."
>
> "Did you do things or organize things differently that weren't just the way everybody else did it? Give me some examples."

I want them to tell me when they went above and beyond and accomplished 104 percent rather than 100 percent.

Hunter Johnson, Director of Human Resources, World Strides:

In determining if someone is a team player, I ask this question:

> "If I talk to your coworkers today, what will they tell me is really great about you and what would they want you to change?"

Usually I hear, "My coworkers think I'm great" or "They think I'm awesome." Although occasionally the response is, "Sometimes I get frustrated with my coworkers because they don't work fast enough or are not accurate, so they would want me to be easier on them." This gives me the opportunity to follow up and ask for further examples or clarifications. That question opens up a door so you can really start drilling down.

I also ask candidates to tell me about a performance appraisal they've had and where they've received some corrective criticism. I want them to tell me about a situation when the feedback wasn't necessarily positive. I ask them:

"Tell me what it was about your performance or behavior that was being criticized."
"Give me examples of what you didn't do properly, and, most importantly, I want to know how you handled the criticism and what you learned from it."

What I'm really looking for is for them to tell me how they grew from it, how they handled it, and whether or not they got frustrated, angry, or upset. I want to know if they took responsibility or just tried to blame it on someone else. This gives me a pretty good indication of how well they will work with others and if they will be difficult to manage.

John Korzec, Director of Human Resources, Otis Elevator:

I always ask people a series of questions about their own behaviors and accomplishments, and then ask them to link that back to the overall impact of the business.

"How did your achievements impact the business?"
"How did what your team accomplished impact the business?"

I want to be sure that individuals know how to relate to the big picture. I want to know if they understand how their individual effort relates to the overall organizational goals and measurements. It's important to determine if they know the link between their activity and how it impacts the organization.

I also use a question that really produces some interesting results. Once candidates are really relaxed and you have developed a good rapport, I ask them to tell me what they like, and I just let them go. I just sit there and nod and write. It's a disarming question, and some of the responses have been remarkable. After they're done, I ask them what they don't like, and tell them their response can be related to business, personal, recreation, family, whatever. I don't want to define it for them; I want them to interpret it themselves. I have used this anywhere from the Harvard Business School to hourly candidates here in our Bloomington plant.

Art Lucas, President and CEO, Lucas Group:

One of the questions I like to ask concerns achievement. I ask candidates:

"Tell me the most significant award or recognition you have received in your career to date."
"Tell me where you were recognized for being an outstanding achiever."
"What do you think is the biggest highlight in your career?"

I want to find out if they truly have any achievements and what do they consider an achievement to be. Another question I like to ask is helpful in assessing their expectations. I will say to candidates:

"If you come to work for us here at the Lucas Group, tell me three things that you would want us to do for you. What would be your expectations? You can be as selfish as you want to be. I really want to know what we would need to do to make you happy in our organization. Tell me three key things."

I'm looking for candidates to tell me what they really want from us, and I have to determine whether those are realistic expectations and whether we can provide them. Another question I like to ask is this:

"On a scale of 1 to 10, 10 being the highest possible rating and 1 being the worst, if I had two each of your peers, subordinates, and superiors in my office, and I asked them to rate you as if you were a product, what is the numerical rating that you would receive from them and why?"

I also tell people that when I do my background and reference check, that is a question that I will ask of their past employers, as well as those they have listed as personal references. That usually gives the candidate pause and they give a very candid response.

Terry Luck, Regional Vice President, Nationwide Advertising Service:

In our organization, the account coordinator's position is very important. We must hire people who pay great attention to detail and are able to cope with stressful situations. In interviewing a candidate for that position, I would ask:

"Tell me about a time when you had to juggle multiple tasks and deal with a high-pressure, stressful customer service situation. How did you handle that and what specific steps did you take to deal with it?"

If the candidate responds, "Well, in the job that I'm in now, I have to do a lot of things, like answering the phone, doing my filing, and I have to be very organized to get my job done," that would not be the answer I'm looking for. If their response was, "Well, earlier this week I had a problem. A client called in and their shipment hadn't arrived on time. We had committed to deliver it on Wednesday by 3:00, and at 5:00 they called me because it wasn't delivered. They were upset and I immediately called the shipping company and I found out there had been a problem in routing the delivery. It ended up in Jacksonville, North Carolina, and not Jacksonville, Florida, where it was supposed to be. I negotiated to be sure that it would be shipped out of North Carolina immediately and delivered to Jacksonville, Florida, by 10:00 A.M. the next day. I then called the client, told them what we had done and asked them if there was anything else we could do to help solve the problem. They said they would be satisfied if it was delivered early the next day. The next morning I called the shipping company to double check on the shipment's whereabouts, and then called the client to confirm that it really was delivered when they said it would be. We dodged a bullet on that one."

This specific response would indicate that the candidate was skilled in dealing with problem situations.

Tom Trotter, General Manager, Howmet Castings:

One thing I like to ask is:

"Please give me a *Reader's Digest* version of your work history. Tell me what you have been doing professionally."

What I look for is how many times they use *we* references as opposed to *I* references. I also like to discuss a candidate's vision of the job. If I were interviewing for a quality manager position, I would say:

"Describe for me what you see as the elements of a successful quality manager and why they are important."

I also want to learn about candidates' own personal development objectives. I'm looking for self-motivation and ownership here. I want them to tell me where they want to go and what they are willing to do to get there.

I also ask an interesting question that helps me to assess the diversity of candidates' thought processes:

"If you could invite three people to dinner, any three people in history, who would they be?"

If all three people are similar, that might indicate a trend of their thought process. If all three people are from different eras and have different achievements and experiences, that would indicate more of a diverse interest.

The Twenty Most Asked Interview Questions

These are considered to be the twenty most frequently asked interview questions. Although for the most part, they are relevant inquiries, exercise caution if you decide to use any or all of them. Because they are so widely used, candidates anticipate them and practice the answers. Many books have been written on how to interview for a job, and they *all* highlight these questions. Seminars and college courses are offered to help people prepare themselves to interview successfully, and they all include practice sessions or role-playing targeted to these twenty questions. The chances are, if you use these questions, you will receive practiced and polished responses! Use your creativity to make them more effective. Use the question design information from Chapter 5 to restructure these inquiries so that you receive the information you want without leaving yourself open to a canned response. If you find that most of your candidates interview perfectly, it could be that you are asking questions that are easy to answer perfectly.

1. Why should I/we hire you?
2. What motivates you?
3. If I were to offer you this position, how do you imagine that you would spend your first two weeks?
4. Other than the ones required, what skills do you have that you feel could enhance this position?
5. Please tell me about a specific area of responsibility that you have really enjoyed.
6. Are you looking for a long-term career or a short-term opportunity?
7. Describe your most ideal and least ideal manager/supervisor.
8. When, in a workplace setting, were you a member or a leader of a team?
9. Tell me about an accomplishment that you are truly proud of.
10. Tell me about a time when you had to go "above and beyond the call of duty."
11. What does your current supervisor do to get the best out of you?
12. How would you define a successful career?
13. Give me an example of a crisis situation you were involved in and how you reacted to it.
14. When will you know that you have "made it?"
15. Tell me about yourself.
16. Why are you giving up your current job?
17. Why are you interested in this job?
18. What do you know about this company?

19. What is more important to you: the salary or the job itself?
20. Describe the best person who ever worked for you or with you.

Unfair Interview Questions

The following is a general information guideline for discussion purposes only; it is not intended as legal guidance or advice. When frontline managers put themselves in vulnerable positions concerning these areas, it is usually unintentional and due to a lack of knowledge or awareness. If you are intentionally practicing discriminatory or unfair hiring practices, you *deserve* to be caught and punished. This information is intended to help you avoid innocent and unintentional mistakes.

The areas that must be avoided in every portion of the interviewing and hiring process are listed in alphabetical order. These are the primary areas in which discrimination or unfair hiring questions can occur. There is a line that cannot be crossed, and probably the best strategy for all frontline managers is not to approach the line. Do not inquire into these areas at all, period! Do not try to finesse questions that might yield this information without your having to ask for it specifically. Whether you agree or disagree with these guidelines, frankly, it doesn't matter. Some may appear to make no sense to you. *It doesn't matter.* Some may appear inappropriately restricting to you as an interviewer. *It doesn't matter.* What does matter is that you avoid them at all costs.

Age: Questions that suggest a preference for persons under forty years old.

Arrests: All inquiries relating to arrests.

Citizenship: An inquiry about citizenship status. (It is fair to state that candidates must provide proof of citizenship, visa, or legal alien status upon being hired.)

Convictions: Questions that divulge conviction information not related to fitness to perform a particular job. Also unfair are questions not solely related to convictions or prison release within seven years of the date of job application.

Family: Specific inquiries about the candidate's spouse, the spouse's employment or salary, children, childcare arrangements, or dependents.

Handicaps: Inquiries that are so general they would reveal handicaps or health conditions not related directly to fitness to perform the job.

Height/Weight: Questions not related to job requirements; any such job requirements must directly affect the candidate's ability to perform the job.

Marital Status: Inquiries related to the candidate's marital status. Also unfair are checklists that ask the candidate to indicate a category representing marital status, such as Mr., Mrs., Miss.

Military: Questions that ask about discharge; a request for discharge papers; an inquiry about the applicant's experience in other armed forces.

Name: All inquiries about a name (or its origin) that divulge marital status, lineage, ancestry, national origin, culture, or religion.

National Origin: All inquiries concerning the candidate's lineage, national origin, descent, birthplace, or mother tongue. (The same kinds of inquiries concerning the candidate's spouse are also unfair.)

Organizations: Questions requiring the candidate to list

the organizations, clubs, societies, or other similar groups to which he or she may belong. Professional organizations specifically relating to the position the candidate is being considered for are acceptable.

Photograph: A request for a photograph before hiring a candidate.

Pregnancy: All inquiries regarding pregnancy, including medical history.

Race or Color: Inquiries that seek information about race or color of skin, hair, and so forth.

Relatives: Inquiries about the names and addresses of the candidate's relatives that might reveal discriminatory information.

Religion or Creed: Questions about religious choices, including holidays observed.

Residence: Inquiries about the relationship of the candidate to persons with whom the applicant resides or the names of such persons; or inquiries that seek to learn whether the applicant owns a home.

Sex: Inquiry into this area are considered unfair. (Gender preference or frequency!)

If a candidate willfully introduces information that may be in violation of these guidelines, do not ask follow-up questions. Respond this way: "That information you just provided may be considered discriminatory or unfair. Neither I nor anyone in this organization would ever consider that kind of information in making a hiring decision. I do not want to discuss it further. Let's move on to . . ." Make sure your disclaimer and rejection of the information is clear.

In Chapter 7, we will look at your real-world needs assessment and offer specific questions to evaluate the candidate in those areas.

7

Aligning the Interview and the Needs Assessment

In Chapter 2 we discussed the importance of beginning the hiring process by creating a real-world needs assessment. In this chapter we determine how to bring your needs assessment to life in your interviews.

You will see the critical areas of evaluation broken down into specific factors with sample questions suggested for each. Many of the questions are presented in related clusters, some stand alone, and all are designed to help you gather the necessary information to predict the candidate's future performance and success.

A valuable tool in helping you increase your interviewing efficiency is an interview assessment measurement. This is a simple method for structuring the interview and assessing the value of individual candidates. For each assessment factor, you will be asked to determine

- The immediacy of need
- Its relevance to performance

- The candidate's ability to meet your predetermined requirements

As an example: If you consider a specific educational degree an urgent must-have, it is assigned a multiple of three. If its relevance to the job is extremely important, it is assigned a relevance factor of five. If the candidate possesses the exact degree you are seeking, he or she receives an assessment rating of five.

$$3 \times 5 \times 5 = 75$$

INTERVIEW ASSESSMENT TOOL

Cheryl Jones	#1 Today	John Brown
Candidate Name	Interview #—Date	Interviewer Name

Skill Inventory		Needs		Relevance to Performance	Candidate Assessment	Score
	Urgent Must have	Train Short term	Coach Long term	Low High	Low High	
Education	3	2	1	1–2–3–4–5	1–2–3–4–5	75

Needs X Relevance X Assessment = Score

Three reasons for this candidate rating.

1. Accounting degree from state university
2. Completed two internships with XYZ Company while in school
3. 3.4 grade point average in major

Issues for pending interview discussion.

1. Pursuit of graduate degree . . . your tuition reimbursement program could be a plus

2. Could achievement of graduate degree shorten longevity?
3. Is there recruiting competition from large accounting firms?

Here is a blank assessment tool:

INTERVIEW ASSESSMENT TOOL

Cheryl Jones	#1 Today	John Brown
Candidate Name	Interview #—Date	Interviewer Name

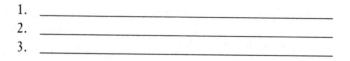

Skill Inventory	Needs			Relevance to Performance	Candidate Assessment	Score
	Urgent Must have	Train Short term	Coach Long term	Low High	Low High	
Education	3	2	1	1–2–3–4–5	1–2–3–4–5	75

Needs X Relevance X Assessment = Score

Three reasons for this candidate rating.

1. _____
2. _____
3. _____

Issues for pending interview discussion.

1. _____
2. _____
3. _____

To avoid impulsive evaluations, challenge yourself to list a minimum of three reasons why you gave the candidate a specific rating. Also, additional questions you want to ask in follow-up interviews, or information you want to provide for the candidate should be noted either during or immediately following the interview. Do not expect yourself to have total recall. This assessment tool will help you to be effective in later-stage interviews, if you are willing to use it effectively.

Create an assessment tool section for

Education	Organizational Skills
Experience	Interactive Skills
Technical Skills	Chemistry—Teamwork—Collaboration
Motivation	

Needs-Assessment-Targeted Questions

Using the design techniques discussed in Chapter 6, the following examples are specific recommendations for interview questions to determine candidates' realistic qualifications and predict their future behaviors and performance levels.

Education

Along with verifying educational claims, it is important that you determine the true value of the candidates' education. It proves they have the ability to set goals and see them through to completion. Does education have meaningful value beyond that? What did candidates learn from their education? How have they put their educational backgrounds to use? Did they participate in funding their own education? Were they serious students? Did they perceive college as a big party? What difference, if any, has education made in their lives?

Your questions may include

"How did your educational experience prepare you to be successful in your career?"

"Have you ever found your education to be a barrier? Tell me why."

"Would you recommend your major course of study to others? Why?"

"What was the most valuable thing you learned in your educational experience?"

"As you look back, would you choose the same course of study? Tell me why."

"Can you list three workplace circumstances that your education did not realistically prepare you for? What would those be?"

"Tell me what led you to choose [college, university, institute]."

"Do you think it's important for students to share some responsibility for the cost of their education? . . . Why? How can that be accomplished?"

"Have you invested in any formal personal growth and development since graduation? Tell me about that."

Experience

Determining the relevance and applicability of candidates' experience is frequently accomplished by using hypothetical and situational role-playing questions. These should be tailored to your specific circumstance and targeted to address situations of either critical importance or chronic challenge. These questions may begin with

"Here's a typical situation we face . . . How would you handle that?"

"Have you ever faced a situation like this . . . How did you respond and, in retrospect, what would you have done differently?"

Other experience inquiries could be

"What are the three most significant accomplishments of your career (or with your current organization)?"

"What are three of your biggest disappointments?"

"If given the chance, what would you do differently? Tell me more about that."

"What do you enjoy most about your current job?"

"What do you enjoy least?"

"If you could change or restructure anything about your current job, what would it be?"

Technical Skills

Typically, technical skills are best determined by situational work simulations. Ask candidates to perform a task that demonstrates the skills and knowledge they claim to possess and that will be part of their responsibilities in your organization. Technical knowledge and computer-based skills are an obvious example. Invite candidates to sit down and demonstrate their abilities to use your system. Asking candidates specific technical questions they would be expected to know the answers to can effectively test technical aptitude. Many candidates claiming technical knowledge have crashed and burned when asked to do a logarithm! Technical proficiency tests administered to all candidates provide excellent opportunities for substantiating claims and separating fact from fantasy. It is important that you ensure the tests are relevant to the job candidates are being considered for and that all candidates complete the same tests. Do not test for brain surgeon skills if you are hiring an admissions representative!

Hypotheticals and situational role-playing questions are valuable in determining technical skills, along with questions concerning problem solving and decisionmaking:

"What is the most challenging task you have to perform? Can you tell me about that in greater detail?"

"What is the most significant problem you have had to solve in the last six months? What did you do? What criteria did you use to come to that solution?"

"What kinds of decisions do you find the most challenging to make? Tell me why."

"Can you give me some examples of situations where you have had to make those types of decisions?"

"Tell me about a time when you've made a bad decision How did you determine it was bad? What did you do to correct it? What was the final outcome?"

"If someone is not technically proficient in your area, how does that begin to show? What are the first signs that someone is floundering?"

"Have you ever felt in over your head? Tell me about that."

Motivation

Motivation exhibits many faces. Are candidates intrinsically or extrinsically motivated? What managerial and organizational support will they need to maintain their motivation? Will you be able to provide the motivational environment necessary for their success? Will these candidates be high-maintenance employees who demand higher-than-average managerial involvement? Do they work well on their own or do they need constant supervision? Work ethic is a core issue; however, many other motivational factors must be considered, including

Adaptability.   How well will the candidates handle shifts in priorities or job assignments? If asked to do something new, will they respond positively? Do they have a "that's not my job" mentality?

Possible questions:

"Tell me three changes you have had to adapt to in the last six months."

"Which were the easiest for you to accept?"

"Which were the most difficult? Why?"

"What has been the most unforeseen or unpredictable circumstance you have had to deal with in your present job?"

"Do you feel you handled it well? If so, why? If not, why not?"

"Is there anything you wish you had done differently?"

"Do priorities change often in your current position?"

"How do you handle those?"

"Just suppose you are engrossed in a task that is important to you and one you really enjoy doing. If you were pulled away from that task to assist in another area that you felt was much less important, how would you respond?"

"Has that ever happened to you? Tell me more about that."

"Tell me about a time you have acted negatively to that. Why?"

Willingness to Take Initiative. Are candidates willing to initiate action? Do they do only what they have been told to do? Can they see the bigger picture and anticipate the next step and accomplish it?

Possible questions:

"Give me an example of a time when you have taken the initiative to make a decision or take an action that resulted in a positive outcome."

"What were the biggest obstacles you faced in taking that initiative? Tell me more about that."

"How do you react when you take initiative and it doesn't go as well as you would have hoped?"

"What's the most significant example of a time when that has happened?"

"When you are working on a project, do you move on to the next step or is it important to get approval before taking action? Why?"

"What do you do if you are working on something and you aren't sure what to do next?"

"When was the last time that happened? What were the results?"

Creativity. How creative are the candidates? Do they demonstrate motivation to challenge their own intellect? Do they strive to find alternative methods? Are they willing to offer new ideas? Do they appear just to come to work, do their jobs, keep their mouths shut, and go home? Will they make creative contributions?

Possible questions:

"What is the most creative suggestion you have recommended to reduce cost, save time, or increase quality?"

"Have you ever received an award for a creative suggestion? Tell me about that."

"I think it's very important for employees to be rewarded for their suggestions, no matter how insignificant they are. Don't you agree? Tell me why."

"What should the rewards typically be?"

"Do you consider yourself a creative person? What makes you say that?"

"When are you at your creative best? Why?"

"What do you do if you get excited about a great idea and others don't share your enthusiasm? When did that happen last? How did you handle it? What was the result?"

Flexibility. Do candidates have the ability to accomplish multiple tasks? Will they become unmotivated or overwhelmed when asked to apply themselves in more than one area? Are they rigid in their structure?

Possible questions:

"What circumstances do you find most frustrating in your current job?"

"How do you overcome your frustrations?"

"What could your organization do differently to minimize the frustration? Give me some examples."

"What does flexibility mean to you?"

"Do you believe it's important to be flexible? Why?"

"How do you determine whether someone is inflexible? Give me examples of that behavior."

"Can you give me examples of your flexibility?"

"Can you tell me about a time when you have been inflexible? What was the outcome?"

"Has anyone ever accused you of being inflexible? . . . Who? Under what circumstances? Was that person correct or incorrect? Tell me more about that."

Ability to Embrace Change. All individuals and organizations are undergoing tremendous change in today's workplace. Most of this is change they don't choose; it is imposed upon them. Some people are able to embrace change; others resist it with titanic efforts. Always consider the possibility that candidates may be applying for employment with your organization because they *cannot* deal with the changes in their current environments. Will they become change resistors for you, too?

Possible questions:

"What has been the biggest change you have experienced during your tenure with your current employer?"

"Under what circumstances do you find it most difficult to adjust to change? Why?"

"Do you think that people are being asked to make too many changes in today's workplace? Why?"

"How do you adjust to change that is imposed upon you when you do not have any influence over the decision?"

"Can you give me some examples of imposed change that you have dealt with well?"

"Can you give me some examples of imposed change where you haven't handled it well?"

"Why do people resist change? Do you experience any of those same reactions within yourself?"
"On a scale of 1 to 10, one being very low, how do you rate your ability to change? Why didn't you rate yourself higher/lower?"

Integrity. Integrity has many definitions; usually it is in the eye of the beholder. Most people perceive themselves as having extremely high integrity, yet see almost everyone else as "integrity-challenged."

Someone with integrity shows consistent behaviors of playing above board and by the rules, coupled with decisionmaking skills that honor constant values and vision. Integrity is demonstrated by what candidates *do* (behavior), not by what they say they do! Keeping agreements is an important part of integrity, along with a track record of doing the right thing even when others aren't around to witness their behavior.

Possible questions:

"How do you define integrity?"
"Have you witnessed others' behavior where they didn't act with integrity? Can you tell me about that?"
"What could they have done differently?"
"Has your integrity ever been tested?"
"How did you react to that circumstance?"
"Is integrity important? If so, why?"
"What are the consequences of not acting with integrity?"
"Have you ever experienced those consequences? Give me some examples."
"Integrity has been defined as 'doing your push-ups when no one is looking.' Does that describe you? Why? Give me some examples."

"What are the 'push-ups' in your organization (the things people tend to let slide when no one is watching)? Do you ever let them slide? If not, why not? If so, why?"

Organizational Skills

As previously discussed, organizational skills are an important component of success. You should consider various factors, including candidates' abilities to plan, to document actions and events, to prepare for a meeting, and to maintain a safe and structured work environment.

The priority of these factors varies depending upon the position you are hiring for; however, organizational skills can be the make-or-break factors separating the mediocre from the exceptional. Effective areas for consideration include

Structuring Tasks in an Appropriate Sequence. Are candidates capable of mastering the challenges and breaking them down into logical, incremental steps? Do they manage their work or does their work manage them?

Possible questions:

"What's the first step you take when you are faced with a new project? Why?"

"Would you give me some examples of when you have done that?"

"Do you ever break your tasks down into sequential steps? Why?"

"What's the biggest advantage to doing so?"

"What are the biggest disadvantages if you don't?"

"Can you give me an example of a time when you didn't sequence your work? What was the outcome?"

"Have you ever had to accomplish a task or project from its initial idea state to its adoption? If yes, tell me about that. If no, how do you think you would handle it?"

Planning.   Are candidates proactive or reactive? Do they have the discipline to create a plan and stick to it? Are they frequently out of control, thereby allowing important responsibilities to fall through the cracks?

Planning also includes experience in developing departmental and organizational plans. Questioning in this area gives an indication of candidates' views of the bigger picture. Do they have experience in seeing things from an overall organizational vision?

Possible questions:

"Tell me about your daily planning. Do you use a system? How do you go about it?"

"What's your strategy when your planning is disrupted?"

"How do you deal with unanticipated crises and interruptions?"

"Have you ever been involved in developing either short - or long-term organizational planning?"

"Can you give me some examples of that?"

"What was the process you used to complete the planning?"

"What was the outcome? Were you ultimately successful?"

"Is planning important to you? If so, why? If not, why not?"

"How did you learn to plan?"

"Does effective planning help you to maintain control of your day? Tell me about that."

"How much time do you spend in planning each day? . . . Why?"

Maintaining a Clean Work Area. Do candidates keep neat and orderly offices or work spaces? Are they able to find things when necessary or are documents piled all over the area? Are their personal work spaces an eyesore? Are these candidates potential sufferers from "desk stress?"

Possible questions:

"On a scale of 1 to 10, 1 being very low, how would rate the cleanliness of your desk or workstation?"

"Why didn't you rate it higher/lower?"

"How does your work area affect your ability to perform?"

"What adjectives would your coworkers use to describe your work area?"

"Why would they say that?"

"What's the biggest challenge you face in maintaining an orderly work area?"

"How do you overcome those challenges? Give me some examples."

"Some people are just naturally disorganized. Are you one of those?"

"What could you do differently to improve your work space? Why haven't you already done it? Tell me about that."

Measuring Results. Are the candidates accustomed to measuring their performances? Are they comfortable with an objective measurement or has their productivity typically been measured by subjective opinions? Do candidates make statements such as, "You can't really measure what I do?" This mind-set can be a red flag. If it can't be measured, how can it be evaluated? When measurements are absent or unclear, candidates generally see their performances as exceptional, but others may have a different opinion.

Possible questions:

"How do you measure your performance?"

"Do you measure your performance differently than your manager measures it? If so, how differently?"

"Is it important to measure your progress and success? If so, why? If not, why not?"

"Many people believe that the jobs they do, and their performances, can't be measured. Is that the case with you? If so, why can't your job and performance be measured? If not, why not?"

"If your work can't be measured, how do you justify requests for an increase in compensation?"

"What measurements could be in place to determine your productivity?"

"Would you be comfortable if those measurements were in place? If so, why? If not, why not?"

"Should compensation be tied to measurement? Why?"

Setting Realistic Goals.   Do candidates demonstrate evidence that they establish realistic goals and see them through to completion? Are they familiar and comfortable with the goal-setting process? Is being held accountable for failure to achieve their goals acceptable?

Possible questions:

"Do you believe in setting goals? Why?"

"What criteria do you use for setting goals?"

"Can you give me three examples of goals you have established that you have successfully achieved?"

"What are the goals you haven't achieved?"

"What is the downside to not establishing goals?"

"Do you find goals motivating? If so, why? If not, why not?"

"Can you describe three long-term goals you have established, two important goals you have already achieved, and one goal with which you are struggling?"

"Some people do not believe in formally establishing and achieving goals. Why do you think that is?"

"Why are some people intimidated by the goal-setting process? Have you ever experienced that?"

"Should there be a consequence to an employee's failure to achieve either individual or organizational goals? If so, why? If not, why not?"

Interactive Interpersonal Skills

To some degree, interactive skills can be witnessed during the interview process. You can evaluate candidates' ability to

- Communicate effectively
- Think on their feet
- Handle stressful or pressure-filled situations
- Establish relationships

The opportunity to make these firsthand observations is an important reason why you cannot hire candidates without face-to-face interviews. However, candidates find it fairly easy to practice the "presence" they will adopt during the interview and to work diligently to perfect the images they want to project. In truth, the depth of interactive interpersonal skills can be easily misrepresented. They can be faked! What you see is not necessarily what you get! Every experienced interviewer has been "conned" by the appearance of exceptional "people" skills, only to find out later that they have hired a direct descendant of Attila the Hun.

As a frontline manager who will have to live with the interactive interpersonal skills of the people hired, you cannot afford to treat this area lightly.

High-priority areas to be probed include

Effective Communication.   Communication challenges are the number one issue facing every organization in today's workplace. Ideal candidates must be able to communicate effectively with individuals, with their peers, with team or work group, and with you as their immediate manager. Effective communication is not just "talking good." They must be able to deliver and receive information that is accurate, tempered emotionally, and encourages positive action.

Possible questions:

"What is the single biggest barrier to effective communication in today's workplace?"

"How do you overcome that barrier? Can you give me some examples of your success?"

"Can you tell me about someone you communicate with effectively? What defines your effective communication?"

"Can you give me examples of people with whom you have communication breakdowns?"

"What seems to be the cause of the breakdowns? What do you think would fix them?"

"Have you ever felt as if you were left out of the communication loop at work? Give me some examples."

"How have you reacted to those circumstances?"

"Can you identify times when you have inadvertently left others out of the communication flow?"

"In retrospect, what would you have done differently?"

"Describe the poorest communicator you have ever worked with. How have you avoided that person's problems? Can you give me some examples?"

"Describe the most effective communicator you have ever worked with. What are the most important things you learned from this person?"

"On a scale of 1 to 10, 1 being low, how would you rate yourself as a communicator? Why didn't you rate it higher/lower?"

"On a scale of 1 to 10, 1 being low, how would your current manager rate your communication skills? Why wouldn't your skills be rated higher/lower?"

Active Listening. Listening is the least practiced skill in America. Most people don't listen; they just wait to talk. Listening is a critical ingredient in solving problems, in planning effectively, in resolving conflicts, and in building high-quality relationships. It is also the foundation of peak workplace performance. You cannot perform exceptionally if you haven't effectively listened to the expectations, standards, and objectives that have been established.

This certainly applies to you as a manager as well as to your employees. One of the major hiring traps for managers is "talking too much." Poor planning, ineffective listening patterns, or an unwillingness to process the communication of others are also significant contributors to that trap. The overwhelming communication tendency in all of us is to focus on getting our point across, not listening to someone else's point of view. It is important that you evaluate this trait in the candidates you interview. Some people believe they don't have *time* to *listen*—a common trait—yet isn't it interesting that they always seem to have enough time to *talk*?

Evaluating candidates' ability to listen effectively is important. Typically, if asked, all candidates will present themselves as having excellent listening skills. Be willing to test that skill; probe to determine the candidates' current levels of ability and their willingness to improve.

Possible questions:

"Are you a good listener?"

"What makes you a good listener?"

"What specific techniques to listen effectively do you use?"

"Can you repeat back to me the last three questions that I've asked you?"

"Why do people have problems listening to each other? Give me some examples of that."

"What are the biggest listening barriers you face?"

"Give me some specific examples of how you overcome those barriers."

"How do you react when someone doesn't listen effectively to you?"

"Can you describe circumstances where you haven't listened effectively?"

"How would your current peers rate your listening skills? Why?"

"How would they recommend that you increase your listening effectiveness?"

In my book, *Getting Promoted: Real Strategies for Advancing Your Career* (Perseus, 1999), the following listening assessment was included as an opportunity for self-evaluation. You may choose to have candidates fill out this assessment, use it as a guideline for developing interview questions, or present it as an oral quiz. The results will yield a wealth of opportunity for further discussion.

Please note that if you ask candidates to complete this or any other assessment, you cannot be selective. *You must ask all candidates to complete the assessment. You cannot treat candidates differently!*

Listening Assessment. On a scale of 1 to 5 (1 being never; 5 being always), rate your listening skills. An honest assessment will allow you to identify your personal strengths and weaknesses and to identify steps for improvement. Not rating yourself honestly and accurately results in perpetuating your listening status quo and maintains significant internal roadblocks to promotion.

I listen as much or more than I talk. _____

I am able to focus on what's being
said without becoming distracted. _____

I listen patiently and allow others to
finish their communications
before adding my comments or
responses. _____

I have a high level of interest in
what's being said. _____

I combat my boredom when listening
to the communications of others. _____

I listen to everyone equally regardless of
position, age, gender, race, and so forth _____

I am always open to diverse opinions,
   especially those different from my own.   _____

I can accurately recall conversations an
   hour after their conclusion.   _____

I give full and complete attention, both
   verbally and nonverbally, to the people
   with whom I am communicating.   _____

I am aware of the nonverbal messages I
   send to others.   _____

I acknowledge when I do not understand a
   communication.   _____

My words, tone of voice, and nonverbals
   are always aligned in support of the
   message I intend to send.   _____

I do not pre-form judgments about what
   other people are saying, and I refrain
   from forming my conclusions until they
   have finished communicating.   _____

I take notes in all important conversations.   _____

I look for areas of agreement and
   de-emphasize disagreements.   _____

Scoring:

Less than 44—significant development of listening skills is
   necessary.

From 45 to 60 is typical—indicating some effective listening skills and room for improvement.

From 61 to 68 indicates extremely effective listening capability.

And 69 plus—look up the words reality and denial in the
   dictionary! Get a second opinion!

Customer Service.　Increased value is being placed on the ability to provide exceptional customer service. Whether serving the external customer who pays for the products and services you produce, or an internal customer (the next individual, department, group, or team in your process), everyone is providing some level of customer service. As we all know, if you are not serving the external customer, you are serving someone who is!

Some people believe they do not have customers or that customer service skills are not a high priority. If you hire candidates with this perception, you will pay a negative price further down the road. People who are not focused on the customer service aspects of their jobs are rarely, if ever, peak performers! You must accurately determine the candidates' skills and the priority candidates place on serving others effectively.

Possible questions:

"Can you give me some examples of the times you have provided exceptional customer service to either an internal or external customer? Tell me more about that."

"Can you give me examples of times when perhaps you haven't provided the service that was necessary? What would you like to have done differently? What did you learn from that?"

"In your opinion, what makes customers perceive they have been treated poorly?"

"Have there been times when you or your organization have contributed to those negative perceptions? Can you describe them in more depth?"

"What makes customers perceive they have been treated exceptionally well? Can you give me examples of when you have done that?"

"Are customer service skills important? Why?"

"Is the customer always right? Why?"

"Do you ever have to deal with customers who are unhappy or irate? How do you handle those situations?"

"Can you give me a specific example of your biggest customer service success and your biggest customer service nightmare? What would you do differently if the situation occurred again?"

Conflict Resolution. Most people *avoid* resolving conflict. They do not see themselves as the cause of conflict and are content to blame others when it occurs. Unfortunately, unresolved conflict tends to fester; relatively small issues can explode into large ones with far-reaching negative complications. When unresolved conflict is high, productivity suffers, passive-aggressive resistant behaviors escalate, and appeals for formal resolutions increase (lawsuits, grievances, mediation requests, and so forth).

Do candidates have the skills and willingness to address conflict? Are they willing to consider the issues of others objectively? Are there indications that their strategies for dealing with conflict are either to flee or to win every conflict, no matter how insignificant? Will they create conflict?

Possible questions:

"What do you think are the root causes for most workplace conflict?"

"Is conflict healthy? If so, why? If not, why not?"

"Are you good at resolving conflict? Why? Give me some examples."

"Please describe the conflict resolution training you have received."

"What are the most important factors in successfully resolving conflict? Why?"

"Why do you think people avoid resolving conflict? Do you ever avoid it? If so, why? If not, why not?"

"Can you give me an example of a conflict you have been involved in?"

"What could the other person have done differently?"

"In retrospect, how could you have handled it differently?"

Risk Taking. Similar to the issue of initiative, risk taking involves taking action when a *consequence* is involved. Are the candidates willing to expose themselves to accountability if they make mistakes? Are they willing to accept appropriate responsibility? Do they tend to make an art form out of playing C.Y.A. (cover your anatomy!)? People who are adverse to risk spend an inordinate amount of time insulating themselves from responsibility. If they spent as much time doing their jobs as they spend creating the defense to prove "it's not my fault," their productivity would explode!

Possible questions:

"Are you a risk taker? Why do you say that?"

"What's the most significant risk you have taken in your current job? What was the outcome?"

"Are you comfortable with risk? If so, why? If not, why not?"

"How do you evaluate whether a risk is worth taking?"

"Have you ever been wrong in your evaluation? Tell me about that. What did you learn?"

"When you take a risk and aren't successful, how do you handle that? Give me some examples."

"What has been your biggest risk failure? Were you judged unfairly? Tell me about that."

Chemistry, Teamwork, Collaboration

The ability to establish collaborative, effective workplace relationships becomes more valuable daily. Candidates must be able to fit in with their peers and to avoid disruptive and antagonistic behaviors that negatively influence the productivity of others. How manageable are the candidates and will they be stabilizing influences on the people around them? This is an area that should be investigated as thoroughly as possible when conducting reference and background checks. Candidates' past peers and managers can be helpful in gathering this type of information. Consider at least ten areas:

Collaborative Work.   Do the candidates work well with others? Are they Lone Rangers who work best only in independent situations? Do they have the ability to bring out the best in others? Are they likely to inhibit the input and creativity of their peers through their overbearing personalities? Will the candidates be synergyzing consensus builders?

Possible questions:

"Would you rather work independently or in collaboration with others? Why?"

"What are the biggest challenges you have faced in working closely with others?"

"How have you overcome those challenges?"

"What kinds of tasks, activities, or projects do you think are best handled collaboratively by a team or group? Can you give me some examples?"

"What kinds of tasks, activities, or projects do you think are best handled independently? Can you give me some examples?"

"Tell me about a time when you were successful in working collaboratively with others."

"How about times when you have not been successful?
What were the primary reasons?"

"What does the term *group synergy* mean to you? Are you
a synergistic influence on others? Give me some examples."

"How would your peers rate your ability to work with
others? Is there anyone who would rate it lower? Who
would that be and why?"

"What does it mean to be a consensus builder? Does that
describe you? Give me three examples of circumstances in which you have been a consensus builder?"

"Have you ever failed to build consensus? Tell me about
that."

Welcoming the Input of Others. Do candidates feel comfortable with receiving input or suggestions from others? Can
they accept critical comment well or do they tend to become
defensive or to dismiss unwanted information? Will they be
willing to accept the viewpoints of their peers or are they always *right*?

Possible questions:

"Are you comfortable when people give you input concerning your tasks? Can you give me some examples?"

"How do you handle the situation when someone gives
you critical comment or unwanted input? When has
that happened most recently? Tell me more about
that."

"Do you feel comfortable about making recommendations to others?"

"Tell me about a time when you have made recommendations that weren't well received? How did you handle that?"

"How could the receiver of your comments have handled it more appropriately?"

"As a professional with your extensive background, knowledge, and experience, how do you handle the situation when other people make recommendations on how you might do your job better? Give me some examples."

"How well do you take criticism? Why? When did it happen most recently? Give me some more details."

"What do you do when you are wrong and others bring it to your attention? Have you ever acted badly?"

"How do you give critical comment to others when you think there needs to be improvement? Give me some examples of a time when you've done that."

"How do you want others to give critical comment to you? Role-play with me; you be the critical commenter."

Avoiding Turf Battles. Do candidates seem protective of their turf? Do they view the organization as a series of separate silos or as an integrated network of connected entities? Do they see others in their organizations as internal customers or internal competitors? What value do they place on the contributions of other teams, departments, or groups? Are they protective of their responsibilities and resistant to allowing others to be active in their spheres of influence?

Possible questions:

"Have you ever worked in an organization where there seemed to be a lot of turf battles or an us-against-them mentality? Describe that to me."

"What causes that to happen? Why?"

"How can these turf battles be avoided?"

"Can you give me some examples of how you have broken down some of those barriers and eliminated turf
issues?"

"Turf battles can be divisive. What creates them? Tell me
more about that."

"Have you ever found it necessary to protect your
boundaries of responsibility? If so, why? If not, why
do you think it never happened?"

"If you were in a position of leadership, how would you
deal with internal turf battles? Have you ever seen
that done?"

Sharing, Not Hoarding Information.   Are candidates willing to
share information openly with others? Do they appear to use
information as a controlling mechanism? Do they enhance
their influence by withholding information and establishing
themselves as subject-matter experts who serve as gatekeepers
of knowledge? Do they share information with a favored few
or their closest peers and intentionally deny it to others? Can
they demonstrate consistent behaviors of openly and honestly
sharing information with others equally? Using information
as a manipulative tool is an obsolete organizational behavior;
are the candidates people who haven't yet received that message?

Possible questions:

"Do you think it's important to share information?
Why?"

"Under what circumstances should information be withheld?"

"How do you maintain confidentiality? Give me some
examples."

"What's the downside to not keeping people informed? When have you seen that occur?"

"If you had the opportunity, what methods or procedures would you put in place to ensure that everyone receives information?"

"Is there information concerning your activities that you do not feel comfortable sharing with others? If so, what?"

"How do you respond when others appear to withhold information from you?"

"Give me three examples of circumstances in which you had knowledge or information that you couldn't share with others, but they knew you possessed it; how did you handle those situations?"

"Why couldn't you share the information in the first place?"

"What defines 'unshareable' information?"

Giving Credit for Achievement.   Are you interviewing candidates who attempt to take credit for the ideas or accomplishments of others? Are they willing to give appropriate recognition to the people who partner with them in success? Do they acknowledge the efforts of others or do they see themselves as the only ones who matter?

Possible questions:

"Can you give me an example of how credit or recognition is shared with everyone involved in an achievement in your current organization? How is that handled?"

"Give me some examples of circumstances where credit and recognition isn't shared? What could be done differently?"

"Is it important to share credit and recognition? Why?"

"Is this whole recognition thing overblown? If so, why? If not, why not?"

"Tell me about someone you work with who has been helpful to you in your success."

"How have you recognized that person's help or contribution?"

"Could you have done a better job of giving that employee credit? If so, why? If not, why not?"

"Have you ever been in a circumstance where someone else has taken credit for your idea or achievement? Tell me about that."

"How did you react to that?"

"Can you look back and perhaps identify times when you have not shared credit appropriately? How can you fix it?"

Establishing Trust.   How willingly do the candidates trust others? Are they exceptionally suspicious or skeptical about others? Do they demonstrate distrust of authority? Will candidates be willing to trust in your judgment and leadership? Are they always looking for the hidden message? Are they consistently searching for ulterior motives?

Possible questions:

"How do you determine whether you can trust someone? Give me some examples."

"How do you determine whether you cannot trust someone? When has that been an issue for you?"

"How do you handle the situation when you are working closely with someone you don't feel you can trust?"

"Is trust important to you? Why?"

"Have you ever given others reason not to trust you? Tell me about that."

"Once trust is broken, how can it be repaired or regained?"

"Do you trust your current manager? If so, why? If not, why not?"

"Do you know someone who is always trying to figure out everyone else's ulterior motives? Tell me about that person."

"Do you ever demonstrate the same behavior? If so, why? If not, why not?"

"Is searching for the hidden meaning really saying that you don't think the information presented is true? Tell me about that."

Treatment of Others.   What are the candidates' thoughts on how they treat others? Do they appear to treat people inconsistently? Is dignity and respect extended to some people and withheld from others? Do you see signs that they are judgmental toward certain individuals or groups? Are they nice only to the people they like?

Possible questions:

"Do you like everyone with whom you work?"

"Give me some specific reasons why you would not like someone."

"How do you work closely with someone whom you don't like? Give me some examples."

"How do you behave differently toward the people you like and the people you don't? Can you give me some specifics?"

"Do you think it's important to treat everyone with dignity and respect? Why?"

"What are some examples of how people are treated with lack of dignity or respect in today's workplace?"

"Have you ever experienced those personally? How have you reacted?"

"Do you realize that you may be treating others the same way unintentionally?"

"What are some instances where that might be happening?"

"How should people react if they perceive they aren't being treated with dignity and respect? Have you ever reacted that way?"

Manageability. Are these candidates who will take your direction and follow established policies and procedures? Have they had trouble with managers in the past? Does it *always* appear to be the manager's fault? Are they consistently critical of their past managers? Do they appear to believe that they are smarter or better than their managers?

Possible questions:

"On a scale of 1 to 10, 1 being low, rate your current manager's skills."

"Why didn't you rate them higher/lower? Tell me more about that."

"If you could change one thing about your current manager, what would it be?"

"Why would you choose that?"

"Give me some examples of how that change could make a difference."

"Describe the best boss you ever had; what made that person great?"

"Tell me about the worst boss you ever had; give me examples of that person's negative behavior."

"How do you confront your manager when you think he or she is wrong?"

"If you do decide to join our organization, what do you want from me as your manager? Can you be more specific?"

"What behavior would drive you nuts and I should avoid? Give me some examples."

"How could I help you excel in your job?"

Emotional Control. Do candidates have the maturity to deal with crises, stress, and pressure? Do they deal with problems by throwing temper tantrums? Do they have the ability to choose their responses to a challenging circumstance or do they give in to knee-jerk, emotional, negative reactions?

Possible questions:

"Tell me about a time when you have lost it at work."

"What circumstances are most difficult for you to handle? Can you give me some examples?"

"Are there certain types of people who seem to set you off? Give me specific examples of their behavior; how do you handle them?"

"What do you do when you are fed up and have had it with everything and everybody?"

"Describe a recent time when you have been in that situation."

"Does that happen often?"

"Give me some tips on how to avoid letting workplace problems get the best of me."

"How do you handle the situation when you see others reacting or behaving badly at work? Can you give me some recent examples? Have you ever found yourself reacting the way they do? Tell me about that."

The Final Question

When you have concluded the buying portion of the interview and you have decided that you want to continue considering candidates for employment, begin the transition from the buying to the selling phase of the interview. The last question to ask before your transition is this:

> "If you could create the perfect job for you and money wasn't an issue, what would that job be? Why?"

You are asking candidates to tell you what they really want in their next positions; then you will determine how your opportunity meets their needs. Listen carefully to their responses and be able to address them in detail. The more your opportunity meets their needs, the greater the chances you will successfully hire a peak performer.

Action Plan:

1. On a separate sheet of paper, write down ten of the questions in Chapters 6 or 7 that will be most helpful to you.
2. List five questions you have been using in your interviewing sessions that you think may be unproductive or missing the mark.
3. Design three new interview questions you believe will be helpful in increasing your interviewing effectiveness. Create your own.
4. Looking back on your interviewing experience, what are three questions you wish you had consistently asked the candidate?

---

*. Harry E. Chambers, *Getting Promoted: Real Strategies for Advancing Your Career* (Reading, Mass.: Perseus Books, 1999), pages 79–80.

8

Selling the Job and Making the Offer

The third phase in your quest to find, hire, and keep peak performing employees is the presentation of yourself, your organization, and your career opportunity to the candidates.

Selling Candidates on Your Opportunity

Although you must try to influence candidates' decisionmaking processes honestly and ethically, with no attempt to mislead the candidates or to make claims or promises that cannot become reality, you also want to make the best impression possible. This phase calls upon your abilities of persuasion. Peak-performing candidates will weigh your opportunity against other offers they have on the table. Highly effective and creative people are at a premium; never make the mistake of thinking that you are the only game in town. You must create a situation where candidates *want* to come work for you.

The Cardinal Rule of Interview Selling

Of primary importance to all peak-performing candidates is how they will benefit personally from working for you and your organization. The key question you must address is this: Why is it in the candidates' best interests to accept your opportunity? What is the benefit to the candidates if they choose to join your organization? What will it mean to them personally? How will it affect their careers? How will it increase their skills? It's not about you; it's about them. The selling phase is not about telling them how good you are; it's painting a picture of how they will benefit from how good *you* are. Selling is communicating "what's in it for them." With most candidates focused on the short term, help them see the benefits of the immediate future. Present your opportunity in incremental benefits of eighteen, thirty-six, and forty-eight months. For many of today's candidates, looking five years ahead or more is looking at an eternity. Retirement plans won't necessarily attract today's peak-performing candidates; however, the immediacy of vesting and the percentage of organizational contribution to their 401(k) and possible stock options *will* attract exceptional people. The future is *now*.

The Components of Selling

During the interviewing, or *buying* phase, the 80/20 guideline was in effect. You did 80 percent of the listening and 20 percent of the talking, and your input was limited primarily to asking response-provoking questions. In the selling phase, the 80/20 guideline still exists; however, your roles are reversed. You will be doing 80 percent of the talking and 20 percent of the listening. The candidates will be doing 80 percent of the listening.

The critical components of effective selling include

The High-Ground Transition. As you change from 80 percent of the listening to 80 percent of the talking, you must develop an effective transition. You want to ease the candidates into a passive role, to focus them on receiving your information as opposed to the more active role of delivering information. Abrupt changes or transitions usually do not work well. Candidates are not impressed if you say, "I've heard enough from you, now shut up and let me talk!" Your transition must clearly, yet gently, signal the next phase of the interview and help candidates realize that their roles have shifted.

Concise high-ground transitional phrases bridge the buying and selling phases; they are connected to a declarative statement on your part and establish your more active role.

Possible statements:

"I have asked you a lot of questions and your responses have been very interesting. Now I'd like to switch roles and tell you some important things about our organization and the opportunity we have available. Please feel free to take notes, and if you have questions, please stop me so that I can explain. I think the best place to start is . . . "

"I have really enjoyed listening to the things you have told me. You obviously have an interesting background and you communicate well. At this point, I would like to present some information about us and the career opportunity we have available. I also want to be sure that I respond to questions that you may have, so please feel free to chime in. Let me start by telling you . . . "

"You have given me a lot of information and I'm impressed. Now I am sure you would like to learn about us and the opportunity we offer. I realize that considering a new job is an important decision, and I want you to have as much information as possible. I would like to give you some background on our organization and where we are going in the future. We are . . . "

Short Organizational Summary.   Next, provide a brief description of your organization. This should be about three hundred words and should describe pertinent facts about the organization, including

Age of the Organization
"We are a twenty-year-old company."
"We are a start-up venture."

Legal Description
"We are a publicly held company."
"We are a privately held organization."
"We are a wholly owned subsidiary of . . . "
"Our stock is traded on the . . . exchange."

Overview of Organizational Mission
"We manufacture pharmaceuticals for the . . . market."
"We provide products and services for the . . . industries."
"We focus on . . . "
"We are the largest provider of products and services to the . . . industry."
"We are the lowest cost provider of products and services in . . . "

Provide a Line of Sight. Describe for candidates how your products or services affect your external customer or the people you serve. It's not enough for them to understand what you do; they must appreciate the result.

> "In providing temporary staffing for the . . . industry, we assist our customers in filling immediate vacancies and address their staffing demand fluctuations."
>
> "In focusing on the banking industry, we develop, install, and service software, ensuring financial institutions the ability to track their customers' accounts accurately. Your monthly bank statement is probably produced from our software."
>
> "We manufacture rubber seals and gaskets for the automotive, aerospace, and agricultural industries. Our products ensure our customers' efficiency by providing shock absorption and leakage prevention. Your car or the next airplane you ride in may contain our products."

Organizational Size and Locations
"We employ 4,000 people in three locations throughout the United States."
"We employ a staff of twenty-five people here in our offices."
"We employ thousands of people in our plants and offices worldwide."
"There are currently three of us in the organization."

Explanation of Hiring Circumstance
"We intend to increase our market share by 8 percent in the next twelve months."

"We have an exciting product launch in ninety days that will require us to add twenty-five more professionals to our customer service staff."

"To maintain our exceptional quality, we want to add to our continuous improvement staff."

"As a result of our organizational realignment, we are adding to our manufacturing workforce here in this plant."

"Because of an internal promotion, we are seeking to fill a position in our . . . department."

Align a "Final Question" Response

In Chapter 7, we discussed the "final question" and the importance of concluding the buying portion of the interview by asking, "If you could create the perfect job for yourself and money wasn't an issue, what would that job be and why?" Whether you use this question or one of your own design, the goal is to encourage candidates to tell you what they really want from their next jobs and what they are most likely to respond well to with your opportunity. When you have determined these factors, relate them back to your opportunity as soon as possible in the selling phase. Follow your organizational summary with a direct reference to *their* issues of importance. You must do so honestly, avoiding the temptation to overstate a reality or to *con* candidates into believing something that may not be true.

The more specific the information you provide in response to their interests, the more success you will achieve. For example,

Promotability. If candidates have stated that the opportunity for promotion is important and they want to know how soon they can ascend to positions of higher authority within the organization, explain the realistic career path and appropriate time lines.

Your information should be preceded by a bridging statement, such as,

> "You mentioned your keen interest in being able to advance within the organization."
>
> "This position is available because the current person has been promoted to a managerial level after eighteen months of service. This is what our employee has accomplished to receive the promotion, and the next step on the ladder would be . . . This is a realistic career path for you if you are able to achieve at a similar level."
>
> "Past exceptional performers in this position have moved into these opportunities within our organization. [List the *factual* career moves people have made.] Typically, these movements occur after twelve to twenty-four months of service, and are based upon the achievement of predetermined expectations. This is what you have to accomplish to get promoted. . . ."

Compensation. If candidates indicate that increased future earnings are most important, outline all opportunities for increased compensation, including gain sharing, bonuses, and so forth. It is critical that you be realistic in your explanations and examples. Exercise caution to avoid being misunderstood concerning compensation guarantees. Do not describe bonus payoffs that no one ever attains as typical. Give probable and possible earnings figures. Unrealistic bonus programs that look good on paper but rarely materialize are soon exposed. Candidates react badly to being "conned."

Possible statements:

"You mentioned the importance of future earnings."
"Last year the average bonus for people in this position was . . ."
"In the past five years, we have had three people who began in this position and reached this increased salary level within twenty-four months."

Increased Responsibility. If candidates have stressed their interest in taking on more responsibility and want to be part of the decisionmaking process, outline for them the current level of responsibility and the realistic opportunities for greater responsibility with the position.
Possible statements:

"You mentioned how important it is for you to grow and expand your responsibilities."
"At the present time, this position entails these specific responsibilities. . . . After you have been with us six months and your performance is meeting or exceeding our expectations, your responsibilities would increase to . . ."
"This position leads to responsibilities in these specific areas. . . . Eventually, you will have the authority to make these [P&L, quality, and so forth] decisions."

If your opportunity truly does *not* meet the candidate's wants, it is always best to acknowledge this as soon as possible. You do not want candidates to be disappointed if they join you and then find that their goals cannot be met. Negative employment surprises of any kind usually result in frustration and anger along with depleted performance, a decrease in commitment, and an increase in the likelihood of their spreading rumor, gossip, and critical comments; a quick departure usually follows.

It is also wise to understand that in the fervor of accepting a new job, people are willing to accept the unacceptable. Limitations or barriers they may see as insignificant now probably will become significant.

Some candidates may tell you they are willing to work for fewer dollars than they are currently earning; however, their willingness will probably change after they receive a series of smaller paychecks.

Some may tell you they are willing to take a job with less responsibility and authority; however, they will soon begin to feel underused.

Some may tell you that they would be willing to accept a position with little opportunity for advancement; however, they may soon become bored and begin to look elsewhere.

Just as you must assess your needs and hire accordingly, you must help candidates assess theirs; if the opportunity is not a good match, the earlier everyone involved realizes and acknowledges it, the better. The best way to assess the quality of the match is to discover candidates' true wants and expectations and painstakingly evaluate the potential of your opportunity to meet their career desires. If it looks like a dumb decision on their part to accept your offer, *it probably is!*

Stress the Effect on Their "Value"

One of the most important factors in selling candidates on accepting your position is establishing how their value will be raised by embracing your opportunity. Most candidates do not expect to retire from your organization; however, they do want to be worth more to themselves, and perhaps to their next employers, the day they leave your employment than they were on the day they began. Identify the personal and professional growth they will likely achieve through their experiences with you and your organization. Candidates do not want to invest their time in positions that will not enhance their abilities, self-worth, and marketability. This may mean acknowledging the possibility of the candidates' short-term tenure and helping them understand how even an interim position with your organization will increase their future options.

Possible statements:

"You may choose not to stay with us long term, and even if that happens, here's what you will learn that will make you more valuable to your next employer."

"As your manager, one of the things that I will promise you is that if you come to work for us, you will be worth more to yourself and to your next employer the day you leave here than you were the day you arrived. I want your experience with us, no matter how long that may be, to be a meaningful part of your career development. Let me give you some examples."

If the potential gain is high enough, peak-performing candidates *may* place less emphasis on factors such as compensation.

Stress Your Organizational Uniqueness

It is important that you communicate to candidates the factors that make your organization different. If you present yourself as a common opportunity, that's how candidates will perceive you. Common is not exciting, and peak performers may feel they are *settling* for a good offer, not accepting a better or best offer. If you present yourself as an exceptional opportunity that is different from any others the candidates may be considering, they will see you as having much greater value.

Art Lucas of the Lucas Group had this to say:

You've got to have a recruiting buzz. We help our clients position themselves in the market to hire exceptional people. What is it about your brand that is going to attract the people you are looking for? Many times organizations really don't understand what that is, and if they don't have it, they had better create it. Every organization, if you think about it, can come up with something that makes them different and which is a unique selling factor for enticing people to come to work for them. It may be they have great tenure in their firm and very low turnover. Maybe people really enjoy working there. Perhaps they treat all of their people extremely well. It could be they have some unique kinds of benefits or flex time. They may have a brand-new product that's getting ready to hit the street that's going to revolutionize their industry. Every company is unique, and they have to identify their brand and their image. A question we always ask is, what is the sizzle within your organization that will make someone come to work there? If you really don't have a sizzle, then you had better be offering a whole lot of compensation. Organizations have to look at themselves differently, see themselves from the candidate's point of view.

Art also added this additional information:

Besides having the right kind of buzz, you also have to have the right kind of hiring process. You have to treat candidates as if they are unique and special. You have got to recruit in what I refer to as Internet speed. We see clients fail in their recruiting efforts and we lose placements because organizations drag the hir-

ing process on. They may want to involve several people who
are traveling in the decisionmaking process, and it may be five
weeks before they can get everyone together. The truth is, that
just doesn't work anymore. You have to make recruiting mission
critical #1. If it's important that you hire the best people to run
your organization and add value, you've got to have a system
that aggressively goes after the right people. You can't treat candidates like a subordinate. You've got to treat them like a customer. When you interview someone, it's like having your number one customer show up at your office. Extend the red carpet
treatment, pick them up in a limousine, put them in a nice hotel.
Do everything you would for your best customer. Most organizations are starting to understand this because the people who
aren't doing it are getting burned. They are not hiring the right
kind of people and they are losing too many good ones. The old
days of "If you're lucky, I'll hire you" are gone.

Establish Performance Standards

The selling phase of the interview provides your first opportunity to establish the high-performance standards, expectations,
and objectives that you demand from your people. Emphasize
that successful candidates will be expected to perform at exceptional levels from the moment they begin working for you. It is
counterproductive to send messages indicating that your organizational standards are low and that the job does not demand
peak productivity. If you somehow imply that working for your
organization is easy and that you maintain a country club
atmosphere, that's exactly what candidates will expect. Peak
performers typically do not want it easy. They want to be affiliated with only the best. Conveying low expectations attracts

candidates who are looking for the easiest way out! If you project the clear message that your people experience high rates of job satisfaction because they are asked to perform to their greatest abilities—and are recognized, honored, and rewarded when they do—candidates will expect to satisfy great demands and standards from day one.

Help candidates realize they are joining an elite organization. Emphasize that they will be considered among the top performers in the industry if they can successfully meet your standards, expectations, and objectives. They should understand they are joining the Marine Corps, not the Brownies or Cub Scouts!

Possible statements:

"Please understand that our performance expectations are extremely high. We pride ourselves in having the highest performance standards in our industry. The truth is, not everyone makes it here. Because of that, showing service with us on your resume can be impressive to your future employers."

"I would like to have a clear understanding that we are an excellent place to work, but our standards are exceptionally high. We treat all employees well and we expect them to earn their way to the table. To be considered for employment here, you must be an exceptional candidate, and to continue your employment with us, you must become an exceptional performer. I have no doubt of your capabilities, and I want to be sure I underscore the importance of turning potential and ability into achievement and results."

"Our performance standards are the highest in our industry. Some people who have been successful in competitive organizations, frankly, have found our expectations to be much more challenging. Although most people rise to the occasion, the truth is, some don't. We expect you to be an exceptional performer from the very beginning, and I assure you, you will be honored and recognized for your level of contribution."

Responding to Their Questions

Listen carefully to the questions candidates ask during the selling phase. They will ask for clarifications concerning some of the information you present. The content of their questions will yield a significant indication of what they are looking for and how interested they are in your opportunity. The candidates' questions will allow you insight into their perceptions of what is most important. Usually, the more questions, the better. Silent candidates are often disinterested candidates.

Answer all questions as truthfully as possible. Even if you anticipate a negative response to your answer, it is in your best interest to deal from a position of truth and accuracy. Strategically, it may be advantageous to delay your answer or perhaps include it with additional information later in the interview. The timing of your information may be important. An effective response could be, "That's an interesting question and I'd like to hold my answer for just a few minutes and include it as a part of some broader information." Be sure you make a notation and *always* follow up on the information requested. If you do not eventually answer the question, candidates will assume you are ducking the issue and they may develop perceptions of dishonesty or distrust.

The Response Model. How you answer candidates' questions is important. You must listen effectively and be sure to respond to the question asked. Overtalking or providing information candidates did not request can be as damaging as ducking or ignoring their inquiries.

To ensure listening effectiveness, summarize what you believe you heard candidates say. They will either affirm your summarization or contend it. Either way, you prove you are trying to listen effectively. If candidates do not agree with your summarization, ask them to please restate the question to be sure you get it right. If they agree, follow up the summarization by offering a compliment about their inquiry and pausing momentarily to consider your response.

"That's a very interesting question. Obviously, that's of major importance. Let me think about that for a second to be sure I respond appropriately." (Pause momentarily, and then answer the question.)

Your compliment affirms the validity of their thought processes and demonstrates your willingness to be open and honest. Your pause indicates that you take their questions seriously; and you buy yourself a moment to gather your thoughts.

In your responses, avoid statements that may unintentionally imply commitment. As an example, if a candidate asks for more money, do not say, "I would be willing to consider that" unless you are indeed willing. Once you make that statement, you have committed to increasing the compensation offer, or you risk indicating that you do not believe the candidate is worth more money. Once you have raised the expectation, not meeting it is a negative. An effective alternative response would be, "I'd be willing to consider your request for more money after you have been with us for six to eight months."

When you indicate a willingness to negotiate further, always follow-up with a specific time line.

Prepare Candidates to Sell the Job to Others

This is an important interviewing factor, frequently over-looked or unrecognized. When interviewing candidates, always remember that people close to them will influence their decisions. Within ten minutes of the end of your interviews, most candidates will be in contact with someone who is eager to find out how the interview went—spouse, significant other, close friend, and, in the case of younger candidates, parents. The influence of these people is critical and could work for or against you; they may be eager for a candidate to make a job change, or they may recommend caution; they may even encourage a candidate to stay put or to accept another offer. If you are going to be successful in hiring exceptional candidates, you must prepare them to sell the job to others and to present your opportunity in the best possible light to those influencers. If they are weak or uncertain in describing your opportunity to others, chances are great they may be talked out of going any further. If they show great excitement and can offer substantial justification to support the decision to change jobs, there is a much better chance they will prevail over negative input.

As you conclude the selling portion of the interview, consider this strategy for testing the candidates' preparedness to convince others of their decisions: "I would be willing to bet that you will contact somebody when you leave this interview to discuss how it went. What are the three most important things you will tell that person concerning what we talked about and your interest in the job?"

Carefully evaluate candidates' responses; they will reveal the three things they consider most important. Not only will these three items provide valuable information for you to follow up on during your next interview but they will tell you what candidates will be telling others! If they cannot provide three compelling things that are important enough to tell others, or if their responses are weak or noncommittal, chances are high that either they have low interest in the job or they will lose interest after the first interview. If they are not prepared to sell the job, they are not prepared to accept it, either. Never allow candidates to leave an interview without determining what they will do to explain or sell the job to others.

Concluding the Interview

Your interview closing will vary depending upon the circumstance and where you are in the sequence of interviewing. The most important factor in your closing is to assess the candidates' commitment to pursue or to accept your opportunity and to determine the *next step* in the process. An effective way to end interviews is to say to candidates: "How would you like this interview to end?"

This closing technique provides the opportunity for candidates to demonstrate their interest by requesting the "next step." Ideally the candidate will respond by saying:

"I'd like you to offer me the job."
"I'd like us to schedule the next interview."
"I'd like to know when you will contact me to set up the
    next interview."

Signs of tentativeness in candidates generally indicate low interest or commitment in pursuing the opportunity. Perhaps they are shopping and not ready to buy! It may indicate a lack of confidence by the candidates or hesitancy to reach out and actively pursue what they want. If candidates want to think about it, to "wait to hear from you," or want to buy time to "compare your opportunity to the others they are looking at," it usually indicates low interest or discomfort with taking risk or initiative.

When candidates hesitate, leave the ball in their court and allow them to make the next move. Chances are great that they will do nothing to follow up and your recruiting effort will be dead in the water. If they do follow up and pursue you, their other opportunities probably did not materialize or they have somehow generated a renewed interest in yours. Either way, it is important for them to reach out to you. Intensly pursuing reluctant candidates usually results in their perceiving you as desperate, which scares them off; or they may allow you to talk them into the job, which rarely generates a positive long-term outcome.

Other closing alternatives include inquiries such as:

"Are you interested in our opportunity?"
"What interests you most about it?"
"What interests you least about it?"
"Should we make a job offer, how long would it take you to decide to accept?"
"Once you accept a job offer, how long would it be until you were able to start work?"
"As our interview draws to a close, is there anything else you would like me to know about you that would be a significant influence on my decision?"

You are looking for high indications of keen interest and the willingness to pursue the next step.

If you decide to schedule a follow-up interview, be clear about logistics. Identify an *exact* time and location for the next interview or when candidates can expect a follow-up call to discuss the next step in the process. Always identify who will initiate the follow-up contact and how that contact will be made (phone, fax, e-mail).

Assign Interim Activity. An additional technique for determining interest and commitment is to assign candidates interim activity. Between interviews, ask them to

- Research your organization.
- Retrieve and forward documentation to verify claims or statements they have made during the interview.
- Create a rough draft of a business plan or strategy for dealing with a hypothetical situation you may propose. (Some candidates may be reluctant to be too specific in their responses for fear that you may be digging for free advice or consulting recommendations.)

The goal of interim activity is twofold: to assess candidates' willingness to participate and the quality of the thought or work they present. Requests for interim activity should be reasonable. Do not expect candidates to do forty hours of work or preparation for the next interview! Small tasks will give you an indication of their interest, willingness, and ability to follow up. Be wary of candidates who forget or don't have time to complete the interim activity.

Background and Reference Checks

An important factor in your hiring decisions is the information you acquire through background and reference checks.

Many frontline managers are either not involved in checking backgrounds and references or willingly delegate the task to others. This is *not* a good strategy. Your hiring decisions are too important to leave the gathering of this important information to someone else. Effective background and reference checks allow you to verify much of the information you have gathered during the interview process and provides the opportunity to gain additional insight into candidates by listening carefully to the experiences and perceptions of others.

These checks are also becoming increasingly important because of the liability issues involved in hiring and employment. If candidates have a history of behavioral or performance problems that should have been discovered through a reasonable pre- or postemployment search, your failure to uncover them could be judged as negligence if you employ them and problems occur that are consistent with their past patterns. You could be held both personally and organizationally liable. If candidates have a poor driving record—for example, they have been convicted for driving under the influence—and you hire them for a job that requires them to drive motor vehicles as a part of their responsibilities, serious legal ramifications could occur if they repeat their past offenses while representing your organization. Usually, personal and employment references are checked *before* you make your offer. Other information, such as credit and background checks, are initiated at the same time; however, the results may be delayed until the employee has already accepted and begun working for you. The discovery of significant negative information can be the basis for dismissal, and it may mean the individual falsified the employment application. Background and reference checks are serious business!

Preparing for Background and Reference Checks

All reference and background checks must be conducted in a consistent manner and the results must be documented. Even if you are unable to gather any relevant information, you must be able to demonstrate your attempted efforts. Most organizations provide internal forms with predetermined questions that must be completed for all employment candidates. It is important to document all reference checks to demonstrate a pattern of consistency. If you attempt to check one, you must attempt to check all. You cannot conduct background checks on some candidates and not on others; that would be considered discriminatory. Also, be sure to ask the same questions of all candidates.

Types of References

Typically, candidates are asked to provide two types of references: personal and professional.

Personal References. Don't expect a lot from personal references. Assume that the references have been primed by candidates and coached as to the information they will provide. Although there are exceptions to everything, most people listed as personal references will give you glowing recommendations! After all, if candidates were not confident that a good reference would be forthcoming, they wouldn't have listed the individual as a source in the first place!

Professional References. The information gathered from professional references tends to be job- or performance-related. Once again, these sources can also be used to learn the names of additional people you may be able to contact. Probably the most valuable information the individuals listed as references by candidates can provide you are the names of additional contacts. You want to discover the names and contact information for

- Past managers and supervisors
- The candidate's peers
- People who have worked for the candidate
- Customers the candidate has served

Please note:

Before reference checks are conducted with current employers or individuals from the candidates' current organization, candidates' permission *must* be obtained. Should there be a backlash to candidates because of your reference-checking efforts, you could bear some responsibility. Most candidates will *not* want you to contact their current employers. Honor the request and delay this reference check until *after* the candidate has accepted your offer, but before the candidate's starting date; this gives the candidate the protection of having an accepted job offer in hand and affords you the opportunity to gather valuable information from the candidate's present organization.

If you have made the decision to hire and receive less than stellar references from a current employer, this will give you an early warning sign of what to watch for during the probationary period. Keep in mind the possibility that a negative reference from a current employer could contain an element of sour grapes.

Focus on Frontline References

Whenever possible, conduct reference checks with the frontline people who have had significant interaction with the candidates. References conducted with traditional staff functions, such as human resources, yield limited information at best; indeed, many organizations today are by policy referring all reference checks to the human resources department. Many are discouraging frontline people from participating in reference checks at all; this limits the information you can obtain. Many organizations now limit reference information to dates of service and titles of positions held. Some verify compensation information, but others refuse to provide anything beyond date and title. Their reasons for limiting information usually concern potential negative liability.

Do everything you can to bypass the staff-based references and contact the frontline people who can provide you with the most valuable information. Again, it is imperative that you obtain permission from candidates before you contact references they did not originally list.

Effective Questions.   Reference checking is similar to the interviewing process; instead of interviewing candidates, you are interviewing the references. Use your creativity to design questions that will be helpful in gathering information and encourage people to talk openly.

Positioning reference questions in groups or cascades is helpful, blends of open- and closed-ended questions being most effective.

Questions may include

"How long did Susan work for you?"
"Which other managers did she work for within the company?"
"Did you choose to hire her or was that decision made by others?"
"What criteria did you use to choose her?" or "In retro-

spect, do you see your decision to hire Susan for your department as a good one?"

"If so, why? If not, why not?"

"Do you have a policy of rehiring employees who have left the company?"

If the response is yes, "Would you consider rehiring John?" If the hiring policy response is *no*, "Would you consider trying to make an exception to rehire John if the possibility arose?"

"If so, why? If not, why not?"

"What suggestions would you offer to help me manage Phyllis more effectively?"

"What could I do to help her be more productive?"

"What tactics or strategies don't work with her?"

"How would you rate Sean's work ethic in comparison to that of his peers? Tell me more about that."

"What are his greatest areas of strength? What are his most significant areas of weakness?"

"If there is one thing you could have done differently with Sean while he worked for you, what would it have been?"

"How did she relate to others within your environment?"

"Does he work well with others?"

"How would you rate her communication skills?"

"Were there any organizational policies that seemed to be a struggle for him?"

"How would you rate her overall performance compared to that of her peers?"

"Did he tend to demonstrate disruptive behaviors? If so, can you give me some examples?"

"If there is one change you would like to see Amanda make in her performance, what would it be?"

"On a scale of 1 to 10, how would you rate Alex as an employee?"

"Why didn't you rate it lower? Why didn't you rate it higher?"

"What are three things that really stood out about Marie, two areas where she appeared to have undeveloped potential, and one thing she must improve on to ensure future success?"

Referencing Past Performance Appraisals

If possible, ask supervisors to refer to candidates' past performance appraisals in your discussions, although be aware that some may be reluctant to do so. These documents can be an excellent source of information. Ask specific questions, such as:

"What areas of performance were rated particularly high?"

"What areas of performance were rated particularly low?"

"What opportunities for improvement were identified?"

"Was she responsive to your recommendations?"

"Did he handle critical comments well?"

"On her appraisal, was Michelle rated higher than most of her peers?"

"How did Mike's performance appraisal compare to others within the department?"

Do not attempt to push supervisors into supplying past performance appraisal information if they are uncomfortable in doing so. However, if the reference check is based on this data, you are not at the mercy of a former supervisor's memory!

Background Checks

Credit and criminal background checks are also helpful. However, they can be cumbersome and bogged down in bureaucratic red tape. Many organizations today find it advantageous to use the services of professional organizations specializing in background checks. Although costs vary with each organization and are influenced by the depth of the reports you are requesting, professional firms tend to gather relevant information faster, in far greater depth, and offer protections against potential liabilities. Laws and policies concerning the gathering of background information change often and differ from state to state. Professional firms are specialists at conducting such services, extensively and legally.

Cheryl Anderson is the Manager of Corporate Services at the Lucas Group. Cheryl has complete experience in reference checking and background investigation. Her comments:

> Having worked for a background investigation firm as the head of Director of Records Department, I was responsible for requesting and consolidating all the criminal, credit, and motor vehicle checks that we would do for our clients. We would also do employment references and educational verifications. Using an outside firm can relinquish some liability. Authorization is made in writing by the client organization to a professional search firm, and this results in a lessening of liability concerning record accuracy. Background investigation firms are responsible for the information they provide. Also, some professional organizations have the ability to conduct searches much quicker and more in-depth. Motor vehicle searches can be conducted nationwide through a background search firm rather than an individual organization having to research each state individually. They have the links and the hookups and employ professionals

who understand how to read and interpret the information they generate. There is also an awful lot of red tape involved when criminal searches are conducted.

Cheryl also believes that professional firms can be helpful in performing employment verifications.

Background investigators frequently find ways to go around the H.R. department. They would go directly to a frontline manager. Many times a manager, direct peer, or past supervisor that worked with the candidate would be more willing to talk to you and share their hands-on experience with the individual, especially if there are problems. You are less likely to hear those from H.R. Typically the H.R. department would be contacted first to verify dates of employment and rehire eligibility, and then other sources would be used, especially if things weren't adding up or there were some questionable areas.

Cheryl had these suggestions for frontline managers who are going to do their own individual reference checks:

One of the things that I think is very important with references is to have a standardized question guideline. It's important to make sure that everybody is asking the same questions. Another very important thing is to document effectively. Frequently reference checks are conducted and notes are scribbled along the margins of the resume. If you review these notes later, many times they are completely incoherent. Also it's important to predetermine the information you want from reference checks. Set all of that up before you even make the first call so you are prepared to lead the direction of the conversation. Ask for your reference contact's name and title. Ask their relationship to the candidate. How many years did they work together? Did they know each other prior to the job or outside of the job? Ask if the reference point was the actual hiring authority. If so, what interested them in the candidate initially? What made them want to hire the individual? What were the skills or personality traits that helped them to make their decision? Also ask if their initial reasons for hiring the candidate you are now considering for employment were ultimately legitimate. Did they get any surprises once the candidate was hired?

It's also important for you to clearly establish your disqualifiers. What background information would result in rejecting someone? You must determine what you will and will not accept within the law in the people you are hiring. As an example, some organizations clearly state that everyone is going to be drug tested prior to employment. There are no exceptions to the testing and no exceptions to the fact that an unsatisfactory test results in the refusal of employment. Standards must be public knowledge and consistently applied throughout the organization.

Correctly conducted, background and reference checks can yield a wealth of information to help you make your hiring decisions. They also help in successfully managing and motivating the candidates you hire.

Making the Job Offer

Typically, job offers are made verbally and then may or may not be followed up with a formal offer in writing. Job offers identify the conditions under which the organization and the candidates agree to form an employment partnership. Plan all job offers carefully; give care to specific information and eliminate the potential for personal interpretations. Eventual misunderstandings will result in someone's feeling misled. Because of the importance of job offers, it is best to obtain professional legal advice in designing or presenting them.

A job offer specifically summarizes

- Job title and duties
- Compensation (including incentives)
- Details concerning performance-based earnings
- Nonmonetary perks
- Moving expenses (including mortgage assistance and so forth)

Some of the pitfalls experienced with job offers may include

- Stating a yearly salary could be interpreted by a court as a guarantee of compensation for one year. It is probably wise to break compensation into monthly, weekly, or perhaps hourly increments.
- Commitments of biannual or yearly performance appraisals and salary reviews can be interpreted as guarantees of employment for increments of six months or one year. It could be held that employment is guaranteed until the time the appraisal is conducted.

Once an offer is made, an attempt to rescind it could become a legal entanglement if the candidates have accepted and given notice or handed in resignations to their current employers.

Successful Job Offer Strategies

Listed below are strategies that increase the likelihood candidates will accept your job offers, keep their commitments to join your organization, and begin successful careers on a timely basis. Many attractive candidates have crashed and burned during the interim between offer, acceptance, and start date.

Negotiate Decision Deadlines. Usually candidates will not accept or decline your job offer immediately. They probably want to take time to consider it and, in most cases, will consult other people before committing. (These are the people they may have to sell the job to!) Never leave an offer open-ended; you must establish a reasonable time frame for them to accept or decline your offer. Three to five days is typically acceptable; extensions should require justification of an unusual extenuating circumstance. Candidates must sense the importance and urgency of making a decision, and you need to move on if they decline. Also establish that candidates are responsible for contacting you when they accept or decline the offer. Do not put yourself in the position of "chasing" them, which may give them the upper hand in attempting further negotiations for more favorable conditions. Make them come to you. If candidates do not meet the predetermined deadline, assume they have declined and move on.

Anticipate Additional Requests

Your job offer may result in a candidate's posing a counterrequest for increases in compensation or other factors (vacation, tuition reimbursement, and so on). This is a common occurrence, and the decision to reopen the job offer for additional negotiation is up to you.

Prepare yourself for the possibility of requests for increases in compensation or benefits and predetermine your limits and responses. Do *not* allow yourself to be backed into a corner by peak-performing candidates requesting increases you have not carefully considered. You may make an ill-advised concession if you have not identified the boundaries of your authority or willingness to increase the offer. Do not make impulsive decisions.

Any increases you are willing to offer may have far-reaching, negative effects on current employees. In Chapter 9, we will discuss incentives and how they affect the organization. Always be careful in the decisions you make.

Frequently, requests for increased compensation are best dealt with through performance-related agreements. If candidates want a 10 percent increase in salary, you may be able to structure an incentive that will give them that level of earnings for the year, but not necessarily in immediate compensation; performance can earn them the income they request through a carefully structured bonus.

Be planful, responsive, and creative in dealing with candidates' counterrequests.

Plan for Counteroffers

Anticipate counteroffers from existing employers. Once a candidate accepts your offer and resigns from current employment, the current organization will probably take steps to keep that individual if the candidate truly is a peak performer. Counteroffers are a common occurrence. Discuss this probability with candidates before they give notice, prepare them for the probability, and jointly predetermine a strategy for response. Do not allow a candidate to be caught off guard by a panicky response from the current employer.

Some candidates are flattered by counteroffers and agree to remain where they are, succumbing to a "Gee, I didn't know you really cared" response. Help them realize that counteroffers are usually too little too late. Convince your candidate that the current organization should not be offering more money, responsibility, or promotion *now* when the candidate is planning to leave if it wasn't willing to offer it without the threat of loss; such an offer is proof that the organization was willing to employ your candidate on the cheap for as long as it could get away with it!

Be aware that some candidates can be swayed. They may perceive it to be in their short-term best interests to stay; however, frequently this works against them in the long term. Help candidates understand that by giving notice and signaling their willingness to leave the organization, they are probably calling into question their loyalty or intention to stay and serve for an extended period. This makes them vulnerable. Although the organization may make a counteroffer to meet its own short-term best interests, its managers may begin to make arrangements to protect themselves from a future defection. These arrangements probably will *not* include your candidates! Giving notice starts the bridge burning, but even if the fire is soon extinguished, you are left, at best, with a weakened structure. Help candidates understand that reality and prepare them to decline counteroffers.

Maintain Interim Contact

The time between offer acceptance and starting date is a time of great vulnerability. Many things can still happen to cause you to lose peak-performing candidates. Counteroffers, remorse, influence from others, and many other possibilities can result in a candidate's reconsidering. It is imperative that you maintain ongoing contact with candidates during this crucial interim time. Don't let a peak-performing candidate get away from you. Although these contacts must be structured around meaningful activity, they should include phone, e-mail, and in-person meetings. The purpose of these contacts is to provide you the opportunity to detect and react to changes in a candidate's circumstances. You want to *know* if your candidate is experiencing second thoughts, candidate's remorse, or has received a counteroffer. You cannot react appropriately if you haven't maintained contact. Candidates won't tell you they are experiencing second thoughts; they tell you only when they have decided to decline!

Opportunities include

- Invite candidates, their spouses, significant others, parents, and so forth, to an informal dinner to celebrate.
- Ask candidates to establish a convenient time to come in before their starting dates and begin the paperwork (W-2 forms, health benefit information, and so on).
- Invite candidates to start moving personal items into the new office or work space.
- Give candidates training information on organizational policies and procedures to review before the starting date.

These are just a few suggestions to encourage you to maintain contact with candidates. Just because they accept on the first of the month doesn't necessarily guarantee they will start on the fifteenth!

Hiring Assessment	**Yes**	**No**
1. Do I understand the importance of *selling* our opportunities to the candidates I interview?	___	___
2. Do I find myself overselling or overstating any aspects about our opportunities?	___	___

3. Do I effectively determine what candidates are looking for in their next job or career moves? ___ ___

4. Do I lose sight of how important the influence of others may be on the candidates' decisions? ___ ___

5. Do I stress how a candidate's value will be raised by accepting our opportunity? ___ ___

6. Do I present our opportunities as common without stressing the unique aspects of our organization? ___ ___

7. Do I establish performance standards, expectations, and objectives with the candidates I interview? ___ ___

8. Do I tend to discount the importance of candidates' questions during the interviewing process? ___ ___

9. Do I close my interviews by determining candidates' interest, willingness, and risk-taking aptitude? ___ ___

10. Do I willingly allow others to conduct background and reference checks? ___ ___

11. Do I maintain appropriate interim contact with candidates during offer, acceptance, and start dates? ___ ___

12. Do I lose some good candidates to counteroffers from their current employers? ___ ___

No responses to the odd-numbered questions (1–3–5–7–9–11) or *yes* responses to the even-numbered questions (2–4–6–8–10–12) indicate opportunities for growth and development.

9

The Use of Incentives and Hiring from a Position of Weakness

The challenges of offering hiring incentives and of recruiting from a position of perceived weakness are important components in the selling phase of hiring in today's workplace. In the past, hiring incentives were rare; today they are commonplace. The health of the economy and dwindling availability of qualified workers has created the need for creative offerings; and with the emerging demographic realities in the workforce, they are here to stay. Effective incentives are an important factor in keeping peak performers.

In the past, high-profile, stable, bricks-and-mortar organizations, many steeped heavily in tradition, have benefited greatly by being able to attract top, cream-of-the-crop candidates. Today, many of these same organizations have fallen out of favor; small startup technology and scientific-based organizations are becoming much more attractive to peak-performing candidates. The lure of potential quick wealth, gained through stock options and explosive growth, has caused many of the best, brightest, and top-performing candidates to shun the traditional and to embrace instead new startup opportunities. The ups and downs of recruiting challenges are sure to continue; indeed, past hiring advantages have become today's liabilities.

Hiring Incentives

Variations of employment-perk packages, previously the domain of high-echelon executives, are routinely being offered today to peak-performing employment candidates. Whether you agree with the strategy of offering hiring incentives or not, they are a fact of life. In many tough labor markets or in tight job classifications, you may not have a choice. "Incentivize or perish" is the new reality. Although not all job classifications demand the use of incentives, the practice is becoming more commonplace and pervasive every day.

Financial Packages

Perhaps most affecting and controversial are the incentives that influence candidates' earnings. Used wisely, they are assets; used inappropriately, they carry a heavy negative downside.

In general, there are three levels of financial incentives:

Signing Bonus. Signing bonuses are predetermined cash sums paid to candidates upon accepting a job and reporting for work. These bonuses have no strings attached; they are merely enticements for joining the organization. It has been estimated that signing bonuses are used from 20 to 30 percent of the time; however, that figure appears to be increasing. Bonuses are offered in the range of from 5 to 15 percent of the starting salary and are influenced by the skill requirements and the overall availability or lack of qualified candidates. The people with the most attractive skills are receiving the highest bonuses. It is a *seller's* market, and in recruiting candidates possessing MBAs, for example, signing bonuses are necessary. If you don't want to pay the bonus, don't expect to recruit those candidates. The growing use of signing bonuses is a reaction to the conditions that exist in today's workplace. Demand is high; the supply side reaps the benefits—a basic fact of economic life.

Signing bonuses carry no requirements of time of service or of productivity. If possible, you may try to structure your bonus offers with performance or time requirements (perhaps a smaller bonus to start, with additional payoffs after eighteen months, or with specific *achievable* performance requirements). If you are able to do so, change the basis of your incentives from signing to longevity or performance. Although these bonuses may be in your fiscal best interest, they may work against you as hiring incentives. Even if you are able to add time or performance requirements to your bonuses, you probably need to offer an immediate payoff to candidates upon their starting the job.

A risk is involved with signing bonuses. Candidates could take the money and run, which is why most organizations require payback if employees leave before a specified date. (This makes a signing bonus a longevity bonus paid up front.) Signing bonuses can also cause internal morale problems with current employees. Understandably, people who have been with you for a long time and have proved themselves by performing at acceptable levels or above are resentful when new employees, untested, are offered incentive packages. In reality, this may not be as prevalent an issue as might be assumed. New employees joining your organization usually do not establish close relationships or develop enough trust in their peers to feel comfortable disclosing their conditions of employment. Although they might tell their friends, they generally do not tell their new coworkers. It takes time for new candidates to feel comfortable with talking to coworkers about personal issues. This does not mean it won't happen; it does mean it happens less often than perhaps assumed.

If signing bonuses do become an issue with existing employees, confront it honestly. Stress that signing bonuses have become the "price of doing business" in today's labor market, and although they may seem unfair to some, they are a fact of life. A few current employees may react by threatening to leave and find their own signing bonuses elsewhere. Although that can happen, in reality, employees who are happy and are experiencing high levels of job satisfaction are unlikely to leave for a one-time 5 to 15 percent bonus.

One-time signing bonuses are usually better than inflated starting salaries. Bonuses entice candidates with the attraction of an immediate payoff, but higher salaries become an escalating cost with each year of longevity. Signing bonuses are paid only once; salaries compound forever.

Signing bonuses should be used to close the job offer. Discuss the salary early, sell candidates on the appeal of your offer, and make them want to join your organization first. Then offer the signing bonus as the final incentive. If candidates are primarily motivated to join you just for the signing bonus, you probably won't have a match made in heaven! The bonus should be the icing, not the cake!

Performance Incentives.   Bonuses tied to performance can be more appealing from the organization's point of view. You pay for what you get! Signing bonuses place all the risks on the organization: Candidates are compensated merely for showing up. Performance bonuses shift the risk to the candidates; they are compensated only if they achieve a predetermined level of performance. Because of this, performance bonuses, if offered in lieu of signing bonuses, should be significantly higher. You may have to overpay on initial performance incentives, but it is worth it to acquire true peak performers. Many peak-performing candidates may be willing to forgo a signing bonus or to accept a substantially lower amount for the opportunity to achieve a much greater payoff based on performance. A critically important factor with performance-related bonuses is whether they are *realistic*. Use performance levels that are achievable. If it takes an act of God to achieve the necessary performance goals, it also takes an act of God to keep the peak performer who achieves well yet doesn't earn a bonus!

Unfortunately, many candidates are skeptical about bonus promises tied to performance. All candidates have heard nightmarish stories about someone who had accepted a job with a great bonus package only to find out that the bonus was completely unrealistic and unachievable. Most candidates are knowledgeable and wary of such hiring tactics. They may even view such offers in a negative light. The worst possible scenario is to hire peak performers who do well yet fall just short of qualifying for their bonuses. The qualifying levels *must* be achievable.

Candidates should also have the opportunity to achieve performance bonuses based on two criteria: personal productivity and overall group, team, or departmental achievement. You want peak performers who are exceptional in their individual efforts and in their abilities to influence people around them. They should be compensated for the contributions they make to the overall effort as well as for the individual effort.

One option for a performance-based bonus is to *guarantee* a candidate's first year bonus, whether it is earned or not. This, in effect, again becomes a payoff for *longevity*. If candidates stay with you through the first year and their performances are acceptable, you ensure they receive their first-year bonuses.

Longevity Bonuses. These incentives are based on *time*. They may be used in conjunction with signing and performance incentives, and they can be valuable in keeping peak performers. Longevity bonuses escalate in value and can be timed to make it in the best interests of employees to stay and qualify for the next bonus or increased incentives.

Longevity incentives include

Stock Options.   These incentives have been previously offered only to higher-echelon executive-level employment candidates. Today, stock options have become standard in many compensation packages. For some employees, these options have lost their luster. Fortunes can be made in stock options when the economy is strong and the bull market is running hot. When things cool, however, stock options can rapidly lose their value. Along with the immediate lure of capital gains, offering stock options is an excellent way to give peak-performing employees a stake in the long-term performance of the organization. Privately held organizations are limited in their use of employee stock options, but they should always be considered in future plans to go public.

Most stock option plans have a three-year longevity. Candidates must remain with the organization a minimum of thirty-six months to exercise their options; future opportunities can also be extended based on continuous service. Obviously, if the stock value plummets, employees have much *less* incentive to stay.

Profit and Gain Sharing.   These bonuses are based on the organization's overall performance. Often limited to for-profit companies in the private sector, employees share in increased profits. Generally, these bonuses are distributed equally to all employees, the lowest ranking classification receiving the same amount as top executives.

Most profit-and-gain-sharing plans require a threshold level of three years of service to qualify, and participation is based on achieving *increased* earnings. An organization identifies a predetermined minimum level of necessary profit increase, its earnings above that level being eligible for profit and gain sharing. This encourages employees to stay and receive their bonuses. Be prepared: The day the checks are issued (typically January 1) might be an exodus day for some!

Miscellaneous Incentives

The following are additional opportunities for creative incentives. Some may be more attractive than others; all bear some downside risk with existing employees. Care should be taken to weigh benefit versus risk. All are being used effectively as hiring incentives in today's workplace. These incentives also have a significant effect on retention.

Accelerating Vacation Benefits.　Reducing the amount of time employees must serve to qualify for extended vacation time is enticing. More and more importance is being placed on recreational, private, and family time, and most candidates highly value the potential for increased vacations.

This incentive is especially effective in recruiting experienced people from other organizations. One of the biggest impediments to experienced people who are changing jobs is the loss of their highly valued and extended paid vacations. When you hire candidates, they receive two weeks vacation after one full year of service, with additional vacation time earned at various thresholds of longevity (usually in increments of five years). If you are interviewing experienced peak performers who are currently employed with another organization, you can offer to match their *current* vacation packages.

Offering accelerated vacation benefits is attractive to less experienced candidates as well. Weighing a job offer from you that may offer three or four weeks vacation after one year could be the deciding factor over another organization that is offering a traditional package.

Some organizations are offering employees up to four long weekends a year (paid Friday and Mondays off), along with their normal vacation packages. This incentive fits today's fast-paced lifestyle of more frequent but short vacation outings.

Vacation accelerations can be a significant issue for your current employees; indeed, vacation incentives may be an issue of more intensity than signing bonuses. Current employees can perceive these incentives as being extremely unfair unless they can participate as well. Sabbaticals or periodic extended vacations may be offered as trade-offs. Potential negative reactions from current employees must be carefully considered in your decision to offer vacation incentives.

Healthcare Benefits. Maintaining high-quality healthcare packages is most important in hiring and retaining peak performers. Health care is a controversial issue in today's workplace; many organizations have found it necessary to reduce healthcare benefits or to increase employees' participation in funding their benefits programs. Although such measures may be a necessary circumstance, some organizations have seized upon current conditions to be opportunistic in saving costs; but from a recruiting standpoint, this action can be pennywise and pound-foolish. Although you cannot offer variations in healthcare benefits or employee payment requirements inconsistently throughout the organization, offering the best possible healthcare benefits at the lowest possible cost to your employees is an effective hiring and longevity incentive. You can position yourself to be far above your competition by offering an exceptional healthcare benefit package that does not greatly increase the cost to your employees. Maintaining an attractive benefit package is extremely important and it can elevate you above your competition.

Educational Incentives and Tuition Reimbursement. Encouraging employees to pursue educational growth and professional development with organizational support is another attractive hiring incentive. This support can be in the form of direct payment, reimbursement upon successful completion, and making the time available to allow employees to participate.

Tom Trotter of Howmet Castings emphasized his use and support of this type of incentive:

> Questions about our tuition reimbursement and professional development programs are frequently asked by candidates that we interview. I think they are exceptionally good draws for the right people. I also believe that if you have people who are interested in pursuing additional personal development, it indicates a lot about their character and their desire to continue to learn. Our way of supporting continued development for new employees is through tuition reimbursement where we help to fund classes that are going to help employees develop professionally and increase growth. In the past three years, we have seen a doubling of the number of people who have taken advantage of our tuition reimbursement program. Some are taking engineering courses in pursuit of an engineering degree, while others may be taking accounting courses, and we are reimbursing employees for their expenses.

I asked Tom whether he saw trends that employees in certain job classifications are taking more advantage of educational reimbursements. His reply:

> I would say that from 15 to 20 percent of our workforce are currently taking advantage of our reimbursement program at the

present time. There may be slightly higher participation from our technical and professional ranks, but I think the production employees are also starting to take advantage. The reason why is that in the past two to three years, we have hired roughly another 150 people and we are attracting many younger people to come to work for us. Prior to that the average age of our employees in manufacturing was probably about fifty. We had a more mature workforce that was not as prone to take advantage of educational opportunities. Today we see a number of our younger production people who recognize this as a pretty good benefit and are taking full advantage of it.

Educational and professional development should *not* be limited to additional college courses only. Any legitimate courses that contribute to growth and development, increase employees' value, and have the potential to have a positive influence on their performances should be eligible for reimbursement under your program. Ground rules for these programs include

Longevity. Generally, employees are eligible after twelve to eighteen months of service. This becomes a time-influenced incentive and also prevents an employee from joining you, finishing a degree at your expense, and then riding off into the sunset!

Commitment to Extended Service. Many organizations require employees who participate in extensive reimbursement programs to commit to a time of extended service with the organization. If they are going to receive a graduate degree that is funded 60 percent or more by the organization, they may be required to sign an agreement promising to either stay with the organization for a minimum of three years after their date of graduation *or* to reimburse the company for its investment. There may be a decreasing percentage payback scale based upon the time of service. This is a common requirement; it is not unlike those imposed upon graduates from the U.S. military academies, who are required to serve a certain time on active duty after graduation.

Flexible Hours and Telecommuting.   Huge incentives in today's workplace. Giving employees reasonable input into their work hours allows them to be sensitive and responsive to their outside pressures and interests (such as family demands); it also offers them opportunities to pursue the other interests in their lives. Although flex hours are not always possible, they demand serious consideration. You cannot offer flexible hours indiscriminately. If you offer them to one, you must offer them to everyone in that classification. It can be a major hiring and retention incentive if employees possess substantial influence over their work hours. Not all, but some jobs lend themselves to telecommuting; allowing employees to dedicate a percentage of their time to working from home can be advantageous for all. Specific telecommuting hours and conditions must be negotiated at the time of hire, and in general, a 60/40 split (60 percent of their time spent at home, 40 percent on-site) is a *maximum* new-hire guideline.

Lifestyle Support.   Many organizations offer attractive support incentives to address the preferences and conditions of today's emerging lifestyles. As examples,
   Health Club or Fitness Center Memberships.   This can be a relatively low-cost incentive offered to all employees that may be attractive to high-achieving, peak-performing candidates. Most local facilities are amenable to negotiating a group membership at a reduced rate; such deals help lower your overall investment. This incentive not only covers a potential cost that candidates may incur themselves, it generates significant bene-

fits for the organization. It helps increase morale, productivity, and may even reduce absenteeism and various health-related problems in your employees. Encouraging better health and fitness yields many payoffs.

Concierge Services Providing services that assist employees with household chores and repairs are extremely popular; they allow you to give your people the precious gift of more *time*. Many organizations offer employees a predetermined dollar amount for services they can use at their discretion. Those services are reimbursed or paid for at organizational expense.

These services may include:

- Laundry and dry cleaning, including pickup and delivery
- Shopping services (grocery and durable goods)
- Minor home repair (plumbing, electrical, painting, *not* including upgrades, additions, or home improvements)
- Pet expenses (which may include veterinary costs, kenneling fees while on vacation)
- On-site auto service

Employees can use their concierge funds to meet their personal needs and to accommodate their individual life styles. This incentive allows them to avoid mundane or distasteful chores and frees time for them to participate in the things they really enjoy doing.

Childcare Referrals. Although some organizations provide on-site childcare, the majority of organizations either do not have a large enough pool of employees' children to justify providing this service or it may be an unrealistic expense. However, it is possible to provide a childcare referral service by gathering information about local service providers and helping employees to be more aware of their options; this strategy can be especially valuable in finding emergency care or in meeting special needs on short notice. Providing this information can also help reduce absenteeism by avoiding the necessity of employees' having to take time off work to cover extraordinary childcare situations (midweek school "off" days due to holidays, teachers' workdays, and so on). Usually the childcare referral service is administered through the human resources department. A similar benefit is the provision of information on local services for the care of elderly parents.

Healthcare Administrative Assistance. This incentive is growing rapidly in popularity and is generally open to employees and their families. Because many people feel burdened by the administrative requirements of their healthcare providers, some organizations are providing their employees assistance in filling out claim forms, dealing with Medicare and Medicaid requirements, and minimizing the frustration of dealing with the growing healthcare bureaucracy, which can be intimidating to many. Provided for all employees, this incentive can be especially attractive to candidates who are involved in caring for their parents or other family members. With the aging of our population, incentives such as these will only increase in value.

Technology Selection Options. Providing candidates the opportunity to select their own computer and technology equipment is an incentive that is escalating *rapidly* in popularity. The brands and quality of equipment used in their jobs has become a badge of honor for many, especially younger candidates who possess high technological savvy. Many employees take great pride in telling others about the types and capabilities of the technology at their disposal. Such pride also affects productivity. Employees work harder to achieve success and to validate *their* selection of the equipment they use.

Hunter Johnson:

> We have found it to be very important to many people if we allow them to pick their own computer and technology equipment that they will be using. It's a challenge that really excites them. If they are considering joining us and know that they can get the latest, greatest, hot computer, with all the toys, bells, and whistles, it's a very exciting opportunity, especially for high-performing candidates who are good with computers. If they are using their equipment in their jobs, it increases production and efficiency if they have input into selecting the technology they will be using. To a degree, I guess it's an ego thing to know that you have the latest, greatest laser printers with the greatest color capability, sound enhancements, and all the other sorts of things that are available.

Obviously, the selection options available to candidates would be limited by reasonable costs and system compatibility; however, empowering people to have some measure of control over the equipment selection process is appealing. Structuring technology upgrades that are tied to length of service can also be an advantage.

Future Outplacement Service. Although appearing to work against your best interest, this incentive addresses the statistically supported reality that peak-performing candidates may not stay with you forever. Offering to fund candidates' use of an effective outplacement service after they have satisfied a longevity requirement (perhaps five years or more), makes you a partner in the candidates' long-term career development strategy. Not only is this attractive to candidates, it provides you with an early warning sign that your peak performers may be considering a job change. You may then have the opportunity to address their discontent. It also allows you to address the challenges of employee transitions. If you cannot retain employees, you will have more time to fill their positions when you know they are conducting active job searches.

Outplacement services tend to be reasonably priced and open to negotiation. They can also be helpful in guiding peak-performing candidates *to* your organization. Candidates will probably appreciate your candor and interest in their overall career development. This incentive can also be tied to long-term performance, with the requirement of having achieved consistently high performance appraisal ratings. You could impose a stipulation of five appraisal ratings that place them in the top 30 percent of your performers (depending upon your evaluation process).

Minor Incentives with Major Impact

Perhaps overlooked, these seemingly incidental incentives can have a significant influence on your hiring *and* retention. Cumulatively, they can have a huge influence on the attractiveness of your organizational culture.

Lifelong Learning. Ongoing life-skills training and seminars on topics such as health, wellness, and financial planning. You might offer consumer assistance, including home-purchase guidelines and legal protections and procedures for dealing with unsatisfactory products and services. Some organizations sponsor programs concerning family issues: effective parenting, college selection and cost planning, conflict resolution, and so forth.

Outdoor Life. Provide walking paths and exercise facilities. Some organizations have pavilions and gazebos wired for outside work and open-air team, group, or departmental meetings (not recommended for organizations in Minnesota or the Dakotas!)

E-Mail-Free Days. Formally scheduled days with no requirement for receiving and responding to e-mails. What a concept! An instant return message can be devised informing the senders that their e-mail will not be received for twenty-four hours and outlining methods for true emergency responses or notification. For those involved in customer service, e-mail-free days must consider routing messages to others who *can* be of immediate help. Under no circumstances do you ever notify customers that they are intentionally being ignored for twenty-four hours! E-mail-free days are a unique and creative way of giving some relief to one of the greatest stress escalators in today's workplace.

Casual Attire. *Every day*, not just casual days. Make it a casual career! No ties or business attire required. Unless an employee is responsible for customer or other external organizational contact, formal business attire may already be obsolete. As we are becoming a more casual society, use reality to your advantage. Business casual is becoming the norm.

Dress-Up Day. As casual attire becomes more common in the workplace, many organizations have found it interesting and rewarding to have regularly scheduled dress-*up* days. Employees have the opportunity to prove to their peers that they clean up real good! Some employees even rent tuxes or wear evening gowns, and really go all out to look their best. It is like bringing the senior prom to work! Dress-up days offer the opportunity to look and act differently; this is extremely helpful in disrupting the tyranny of repetition that engulfs many people in today's organizations.

Do-Something-Different Day. In keeping with the theme of disrupting repetitious behaviors and tasks, provide periodic opportunities for employees to learn additional skills and perform different jobs within the organization. If employees work in the office in a white-collar environment, let them spend certain days in the warehouse. If employees work in the lab, provide them the opportunity to accompany sales people out in the field to see the world from a different perspective. These opportunities also have a great effect on productivity. Along with reducing boredom, employees learn to understand and value the contributions of others and become more aware of the difficulty and importance of other people's jobs. This awareness results in less of the predictable "us against them" organizational mentalities that sometimes develop; and their increased awareness raises the importance of the tasks they do in the service of others.

Organizationally Sponsored Adventure Travel. Organizationally funded adventure or educational travel is an incentive that is also growing in popularity. Raft trips, hiking adventures, archeological digs, art study tours, and so forth, all of which are targeted to the individual employee's age and interest, can be interesting. Allowing employees to choose their *own* adventures is generally more attractive than predetermining one event for all. Giving employees opportunities to participate in unusual learning and adventure events with their peers improves morale, increases teamwork, and contributes to an increasingly bonded culture; it also promotes retention.

Recruiting from a Position of Weakness

Many frontline managers believe they are at a recruiting disadvantage and believe that other industries or organizations may be better positioned to attract the brightest and best of the available peak-performing candidates. In reality, this may be true. At any given time, hot jobs, hot industries, or hot organizations do have recruiting advantages; finding attractive candidates is much easier for them than it may be for others. Although these windows of recruiting opportunity tend to be cyclical and short-lived, they do exist. If you are facing a perceived or real recruiting disadvantage, stay focused on these three hiring realities:

1. You cannot land every candidate! It is a fact of life that not every candidate will find you, your organization, or your recruiting package attractive. You cannot win them all and, yes, some highly attractive candidates are going to flock to the current hot situation like a moth to a bright light. It also stands to reason that you are not going to lose them all either! There are a high percentage of candidates who will find your organization and offer appealing. Do not give up until you find them. Candidates are looking for many different things, and not everyone is attracted to the biggest or most visible employers of the moment. It is your job to discover what candidates want and present your opportunity to meet their needs! Do not put yourself at the mental disadvantage of perceiving that what you have to offer won't land some of the best. Do not become your own worst enemy. You won't get them all, but you will get some. The truth is, you don't need to

hire an army of peak performers, you need only a valuable *few*.

2. All organizations have weaknesses! All organizations, no matter how big or attractive they or their industry might be have soft underbellies of vulnerability. Many candidates have found that if the job offer looks too good to be true, it's probably not true. Joining the largest organization in a particular industry can result in exceptional candidates' being lost among the herd. They may end up being only one of the many. The attractiveness of certain industries can plummet with unforeseen speed. The draw of the high-tech dot coms soured for many as the reality of economics and the stock market reasserted themselves. The lure of quick riches can leave candidates with nothing more than an interesting addition to their resumes and a story to be told. The appeal of industry-dominant organizations has waned as rightsizing, downsizing, upsizing, reorganization, restructuring—or whatever the euphemism of the moment is for eliminating jobs—have taken their toll. Head-count reductions have affected *all* segments of the economy. The dragon of recruiting and hiring dominance is a dragon that can be slain.

3. The strengths and appeal of your offer! The quality and unique aspects of you, your organization, and your offer will appeal to many. If you truly focus on providing an excellent employment opportunity and relate your offer to the candidates' self-interest, you will be able to recruit and hire effectively in competition with the dominant players.

As Art Lucas said, you must develop your "hiring buzz" thoughtfully. For example, candidates may have a much larger and quicker effect in your organization than they would on a larger organization. Rather than joining a dominant technology giant, they can bring their skills and expertise to your more acute technology needs. They can be the leaders, or the go-to persons, rather than merely members of the flock. Instead of being the developing "wanna be" people with another organization, they can be already doing it with yours! Perhaps they can achieve "been-there-done-that" status much more quickly within your organization.

Candidates who find one of the big accounting firms attractive may have the opportunity to learn more and develop faster within your smaller accounting environment. Rather than risk being put in a niche in a larger organization, they can experience much greater exposure within yours because it may be necessary to learn and perform more aspects of their jobs.

You have many counteroptions available to you in recruiting from a position of weakness, including

Heritage and Stability

If you are not exciting and new, stressing your heritage, history, success, and longevity can be an attractive counter. The instability and risk inherent with new startups or trendy organizations and industries won't be appealing to all. Bricks and mortar have their strength! No doubt many candidates are attracted to new high-risk opportunities, but others welcome the comfort and security of a long-term track record of stability.

Dot coms come and dot coms go. Do not discount the importance of stability, longevity, and tradition for many peak-performing candidates.

John Korzec of Otis Elevator Company has this to say:

You have to take the time and discern what the assets and attractive features of your company are. That's a very individual thing. I emphasize our global presence and our association with the United Technologies Corporation. I emphasize the very diverse range of opportunities that we have at Otis, ranging from manufacturing to sales to service and construction, and the opportunity to interact with people in all of those environments. I tell candidates they can go to the job site and interact with the lunch-pail set and they can be in the most elaborate boardroom in America, dealing with some of the richest developers in the country. For many, that's exciting. While we are not the dot coms and not considered high-tech, we do have many elements that make us a very exciting company. We are entering e-commerce and they are going to be able order an elevator over the Internet and spec out an elevator electronically. Elevators are going to be equipped with digital displays of information coming from the Internet in the very near future. There are some things that are very unique about our company, and I tell people about our heritage. We are almost 150 years old, and that indicates we must be doing something right. Every company has attractive features, and it's not just the economic package that they have to offer. Find your strengths and stress them, whether it's global presence, diversity of opportunity, or whatever, you need to emphasize those areas.

Immediate Impact and Increased Value

Realizing that many peak-performing candidates will *not* have an extended longevity with your organization (beyond six years), engage them in discussions concerning their next possible career move. Joining your organization and performing to the best of their abilities will allow them to gain knowledge, experience, and growth, perhaps far sooner than in larger, potential career-stifling organizations. The experience they gather from your organization may well position them for a more attractive and lucrative next step. Once again, peak-performing candidates will appreciate your candor and may respond well to your thoughts on career planning. It is natural for you to hope peak-performing candidates will stay with you forever, yet the reality indicates they won't. Emphasize your potential to raise their market value sooner! Making a legitimate commitment to candidates and helping to position them for future career growth, either inside or outside your organization, will help blunt some of the attractiveness of more dominant, glamorous organizations. A couple of years experience with a well-known organization looks good on their resumes, but it does lump them in with a large group of people who have followed the same track. A proven track record of achievement and growth within your organization may help to define their uniqueness for future employers and position them above the pack.

The Opportunity to Lead Change

Many startup organizations, especially in fast-paced high-tech environments, entice certain peak-performing candidates by offering ground-floor, entry-level situations coupled with the opportunity to create something. Many people find it attractive to be involved in the creation or birth of an organization and to watch it grow; it is also attractive for others to be involved in later stages of organizational development. The opportunity to take the creation and success of others, grow it, and change it to meet the current economic challenges is an appealing enticement. The potential to lead second-generation change can be more attractive than ground-floor startup opportunities. For some, continuation is more challenging than creation!

Stress the opportunity for candidates to be involved in significant organizational change and the potential to influence the direction and impact of that change. Different candidates are attracted to different levels of challenge, and your organization will be able to offer an attractive opportunity to a segment of the peak-performing candidates currently available. Do not sell yourself or your organization short.

Hiring Assessment

Phase One:

- What are the current hiring incentives we offer?
- Are they effective?
- Have I/we analyzed the cost/benefit relationships for these incentives?

Phase Two:

- What additional incentives could we offer?
- Would we be willing to increase our investment in incentives *if* we attracted and hired better candidates?
- If so, how much more could we invest?
- If not, why not?

Phase Three:

- What incentives are our competitors offering?
- Are they hiring better candidates?

- Where are our competitors vulnerable in their hiring offers?

Phase Four:

- Do I perceive I/we are at a recruiting disadvantage? Why?
- What are the unique strengths of our organization?
- How can the decision to join us accelerate a peak-performing candidate's career?
- How can candidates bring change or have an immediate effect within our organization?

PART THREE

Keeping Peak Performers

10

Creating the
Culture of Retention

The final phase of finding, hiring, and keeping peak performers is skill development and retention. Once you have successfully hired employees who perform at exceptional levels, you want to develop them by increasing their skills and abilities. You want to yield the maximum amount of performance from them for as long as possible. Successfully hiring peak performers does not guarantee that you will keep them forever. Retaining their services for an extended period is a realistic goal. Instead of an employment period of two years, it means extending to four. Instead of four years, it means keeping them for six or seven. The longer you keep peak-performing employees, the more value you derive from their services. Not only do you reap a much greater yield from their productivity but you dramatically reduce your recruiting, hiring, and replacement costs. Hiring five people in ten years to fill the same job due to constant turnover is much more costly and less efficient than hiring one or two!

To achieve these levels of advanced skill development and to keep peak performers longer, the organization must create and maintain a "culture of retention." Just as you, the frontline manager, have a tremendous influence on the development and longevity of the employee, the organizational environment and culture play an equally critical role.

The organizational culture encompasses the overall values that are determined to be most important, and the willingness to support those values through the investment of resources, creation of effective policies, and the reinforcement and rewarding of appropriate behaviors. The difference between *statements* or *intentions* of culture and the enabling and nurturing of these professed values is a journey of thousands of miles.

Many organizations suffer from the gulf that exists between what they say they will do and what they really do! If your organization refuses to invest in training or to maintain compensation packages equal to your competition, developing and retaining employees is a near impossible task. The organization must walk its talk. If your organization treats people as commodities or interchangeable parts and not as valuable contributors to the overall organizational success, you will have difficulty in developing and retaining employees. If employees are not treated with dignity and respect, do not assume they will perform at exceptional levels and stay with you long term.

To create the culture of retention, your organization must establish, communicate, support, nurture, and reinforce definite cultural values.

The Culture of Preparation

Employees must constantly be prepared to address the emerging challenges of today's and tomorrow's workplace. You must provide the ongoing support of continuous personal and organizational growth and improvement. Because the demands of the workplace are constantly changing and the external economic challenges to the organization are always being redefined, employees must be prepared to meet such escalating demands and challenges. Survival and success today demand the acknowledgement that the procedures and behaviors that brought you to where you are today will not take you where you want to go tomorrow. Everyone must be prepared to do things differently.

Several factors contribute to the culture of preparation.

Training

One of the foundations of preparation is training. Skill development and productivity increase when training needs are assessed and met effectively. Training raises employees' value, always important to today's peak performers.

No matter how exceptional your employment candidates may be, they carry negative baggage from their previous experiences. Position yourself to capitalize on their strengths, eliminate their bad habits, and help them overcome existing performance weaknesses—all accomplished through effective training.

Unfortunately, many organizations see training as a necessary evil to be addressed reluctantly and with minimal effort, resources, and time. Often the organization believes that we do not have time to train our people, yet we always have time to fix ongoing problems. Most organizations do not experience many new problems; they tend to deal with the same ones repetitively because they do not train their employees to do things differently!

Some organizations perceive that hiring experienced people is a valid justification for providing little or no training. Many frontline managers are guilty of the shortsighted opinion that "If I hire good, experienced people, I won't have to put a lot of time and effort into training." In truth, the organization pays a high price for withholding effective training. Chief among the costs is the failure to increase skill levels or to correct existing flaws in process or performance. For example, in economic downturns or when certain industries or organizations go through tough financial times, training is one of the first areas affected negatively. Budget cuts hit training departments first. You may save dollars today by not training; however, you will pay a high price in the future when productivity falls, quality suffers, and new technology is not used to its greatest potential. Failing to prepare your employees to do things differently guarantees a continuation of today's results and outcomes with impending obsolescence!

Peak performers thrive on training. They do not think they know it all or that they do not need training. Far from it. Exceptional performers can never get enough training. They do not say, "I'm good enough, leave me alone." They tend toward "I'm good, and I want to get better." Peak performers seek increased knowledge and skills and they welcome being held to increased performance post-training expectations. Organizations and managers who value and support training yield much greater levels of performance from their people and experience significantly less turnover.

Do not allow yourself or your organization to fall into the trap of hiring peak performers and then training them to mediocrity.

Initial Training. No matter how much experience the peak performers you hire may possess, or how exceptional their past productivity has been, they *must* receive thorough initial training when they join your organization. No matter how much they know or how good they are, your organization does things differently from the candidates' previous employers.

They must receive training on organizational policies and procedures, and be introduced to your processes and standards of quality. Peak performers will excel at adopting your current processes and procedures if they know what they are! Do not assume they already know. To hire peak performers and not train them effectively is a terrible waste of valuable resources.

By not providing appropriate initial training for peak-performing candidates, you send a series of negative messages, including

"You are not worth the dedication of time or resources to develop your skills."

"The quality of your performance really doesn't matter."

"We hired you to continue to do the tasks just the way you have always done them."

"We have little confidence in our standards, processes, or policies, and we just want you to wing it."

When new peak-performing employees make statements such as, "Well, that's the way we used to do it over at the ABC Company," they are sending you the message that you have not presented them new behaviors for success in your environment. You have probably given them the strong impression that they are expected to do it the way they've always done it.

No New Responsibilities Without Training.   Never ask peak-performing employees to accept additional delegated tasks, new assignments, or increased responsibilities without providing them the appropriate training. If you train them properly, they will perform well; if you do not, they will perform poorly, they will be frustrated, and they will produce negative results. If you don't train them, you invite failure. Peak performers want to succeed. Do not put them in circumstances where the likelihood of failure or low achievement is increased because of your lack of training support.

Focus Training on Current Technology. Always support peak-performing employees in continuing to develop their technological skills. Peak performers want to be challenged and they want to learn; if they feel that their growth, development, or exposure to current technology is being retarded, they look elsewhere for greater opportunity. If new technology is available, they want it. When upgrades are adopted, they want to be on top of them. Peak performers deplore being in a position of technological disadvantage. If they think they are not learning enough or they are falling behind the technological learning curve because of the unavailability of new skills and information, they will be gone!

Identify Their Skills of Choice. In conjunction with the training, growth, and development necessary to perform their current and future tasks and responsibilities, be keenly aware of the additional skills your peak-performing employees want to develop in themselves. For example, you may have exceptional employees in your production area who want to increase their knowledge of the financial aspects of your business or industry, or perhaps become experts in environmental health and safety issues. Do everything possible to support their interests and help them receive training in the areas that are important to them. Many employees want to become specialists in certain aspects of their responsibilities. Support them in developing their expertise and be willing to provide training even if it appears to go beyond current needs. Their enthusiasm to learn and your willingness to support them create a synergism that works in everyone's best interest!

Training to Prepare for the Next Level. Training also proves to peak-performing employees that you support them in expanding their responsibilities. Your willingness to invest in them creates the foundation to support a longer team relationship. For those who indicate a desire to move into management, provide basic management training to prepare them for future opportunities. Although you cannot guarantee they will become managers, you can help them prepare to compete for future managerial positions. Encourage your employees to earn this type of training through their current exceptional performances. You can establish a quid pro quo for their meeting or exceeding expectations. If peak-performing employees meet or surpass their productivity goals, agree that you will, in turn, provide the training they need for career growth. If they do not meet their performance goals, they are not proving themselves deserving of future promotion; if they do meet them, support them in pursuit of their long-term goals.

Expand Training to External Sources. Do not limit your peak-performing employees' growth and development only to the in-house training efforts of your organization. Those efforts may be exceptional, but peak-performing employees are often interested in external opportunities as well. These opportunities may be in the form of tuition reimbursement programs or through external learning opportunities that are not necessarily degree programs. External opportunities include seminars and programs offered through the business development offices of local colleges and universities and training for certification through professional associations.

Supporting external opportunities means a double-tiered investment for your organization. Not only do you pay the expenses for the training, you also lose employees' productivity during their training time. Generally, these investments are well worth making.

A general guideline for peak-performing employees is a minimum of forty hours per year of training (combined internal and external), with the equivalent of 10 percent of their gross compensation reinvested in their growth and development. (An employee making $50,000 per year should receive a minimum of $5,000 of training.) Failing to invest in peak performers usually means you invest in finding and hiring their replacements!

Continuous Process Improvement

The culture of preparation includes preparing the organization as well as the employees to improve their performances and move into the future. Regardless of the nature of your organization or the segment of the economy you represent, the external challenges of economy and quality that you face are escalating each day. The demand for more efficiencies, the profitability, and the expectations of increasing cost and quality of those who use your products or services, are changing at a dramatic rate unparalleled in our economic history.

Peak-performing employees want to be affiliated with peak-performing organizations. If they think your organization is stagnant, hesitant, or unwilling to improve your processes constantly, they soon become disenchanted. Exceptional employees do not stay in environments that appear to invite obsolescence.

Your process improvement efforts must be continuous and visible to your employees. They must observe tangible efforts of improvement from the organization. Their expectations of you are as high as yours are of them!

Delegate into Their Strengths

The peak performers you hire possess multiple skill strengths and abilities. Prepare them for future growth and allow them to experience ongoing success by delegating into those strengths. Provide them with as many tasks and challenges as possible that allow them to showcase their abilities. Many of the tasks you may currently be performing can be delegated to your peak performers. They may not initially complete the tasks as well as you do, but they can soon develop high competence. The truth is, you couldn't do the tasks effectively, either, until you were given the opportunity. Pass that same opportunity for growth along to them. Prepare them to achieve even more by giving them additional challenges within their current capabilities. Identify what they do well and give them more of it!

When delegating tasks to peak performers, make sure that they understand why they are being asked to do them. When they realize that some tasks are being assigned to them to help showcase their abilities and increase their influence on overall productivity, they will be highly motivated to perform successfully. Delegating into their strengths can reward you with the wonderful gift of time. Tasks you assign to them may be those you do not need to continue doing; you can be free to address more important activities.

As mentioned previously, peak performers want to be worth more the day they leave your organization than they were the day they began their employment. They want to be worth more to themselves, having gained confidence and personal satisfaction in knowing they have performed well. They want to increase their inventory of skills, expand their future options, and be worth more to a potential future employer. They want to command greater rates of compensation and positions of expanded responsibilities. Peak-performing employees who are accelerating their learning, experiencing high personal growth, and preparing for greater future achievement will extend their time of service to continue their learning and development. Even in the face of other opportunities, employees who believe their value is being significantly increased will not leave you for small compensation increases. If someone offers to double your peak performers' compensation, however, they will choose to move on (frankly, so would we all). However, barring significantly greater earnings, employees who feel valued and experience an accelerated pace of learning and development through effective preparation tend to stay where they are. You can accomplish retention by creating a culture of preparation.

The Culture of Inclusion

Peak performers want to make a contribution. They are not content with coming to work, being good boys and girls, doing their jobs, and going home. They are not just in it for the paycheck. Job satisfaction for these employees is typically defined as the opportunity to do meaningful work, have influence in the decisions that affect their areas of interest, and to make a difference in the organization. They want to be included and valued. If they feel excluded or separated from the mainstream activities of the organization, they will probably begin to seek new opportunities for increased influence.

Cultures of inclusion emphasize

Listening

Peak performers want to be listened to. They take high interest in their responsibilities and think of ways to improve their performances and have a positive influence on organizational procedures and processes. They think about what is happening, and their thought processes extend beyond their current responsibilities. They may have ideas on how to improve other areas of the organization, and they want their ideas listened to. If they believe their observations and ideas are not included or considered in planning and decisionmaking, they experience frustration and sometimes anger. They do not expect you to adopt all their ideas automatically; however, they do expect you to listen and consider them!

Some critical factors of listening are

Availability.   You must be available if you are going to listen. Peak performers must have access not only to their frontline managers but also to other influential people in the organization. It is not enough to have an open-door policy; when the door is open, somebody must be home!

If peak performers do not have frequent opportunities to share their thoughts with others, they will search for employment where they will have those opportunities.

Feedback Mechanisms.   Not every idea generated by peak performers can be adopted or included in future plans. Some of their suggestions will be without merit, others may be beyond the scope of the organization's capabilities, and some may require resources that are unavailable or unrealistic. Probably two out of three of their suggestions may not be usable for various reasons; however, even though you may not act upon some of their suggestions, you must respond to them. You must develop systematic feedback for informing employees of the disposition of their ideas.

Feedback on ideas is appropriately provided within forty-eight to seventy-two hours, or two to three workdays after they were received. Even when you reject suggestions from employees, they need to be told why. Although they will probably disagree with you, they will appreciate your listening, considering their ideas or suggestions, and responding to them. Ignoring their input is a real bad thing!

Take the time to consider their input honestly. Do not reject peak performers' suggestions out of hand with such knee-jerk reactions as

"No, that will never work."

"No, we tried that ten years ago. It didn't work then and it won't work now."

"No, upper management would never consider that."

These types of responses prove only that you do not value your employees or their input. How can you value it if you are not even willing to think about it? Even if you do not give a concrete response after seventy-two hours, let the peak performers know that you are still considering their ideas and provide them with updates until you reach a decision.

Always initiate the feedback. Never make peak performers chase you to find out the results of their suggestions.

Provide Incremental Increases of Responsibility

In today's workplace, organizations are flatter, leaner, and more streamlined; everyone is being asked to do more with less. There are fewer opportunities for promotion. Most organizations have fewer management positions available, being reluctant to create new positions or even fill vacancies without carefully considering other opportunities. The career path of achieving multiple promotions may not be available to all peak-performing employees. Even though they may be deserving of promotion, you must have positions to promote them into! In the past, organizations created positions for people just because they deserved promotion. Such policy contributed to the bloating of many organizations; however, some of this bloating has been relieved through rightsizing, downsizing, head-count reductions, and so forth. The bottom line is that you may not be able to retain peak-performing employees by offering ongoing promotional opportunities. Even if you want to promote them and they deserve it, promotion may not be a realistic alternative.

You can continue to challenge peak-performing employees and further include them in organizational influence with periodic increases in their responsibilities, however. These increases can often be identified and timed in advance. Initial levels of responsibility can be increased incrementally at predetermined times (six months, twelve months, eighteen months, and so on), with specific identification of what the increased influence and decisionmaking responsibilities will be. This strategy allows employees to see that they are playing an increasingly important role and being included in organizational plans for growth.

There is another major advantage to incrementally increasing responsibilities. Peak-performing employees often become bored or feel stagnant if they are not continuously challenged. Once tasks and responsibilities are mastered, they soon become repetitious. Repetition feeds boredom. Boredom is deadly for peak performers. Familiarity breeds contempt, and familiarity, through lack of challenge, encourages peak performers to move on. Keep them challenged by increasing their responsibilities.

Avoid Overload. Providing incremental increases in responsibilities also has downside risk. Take care to balance new responsibilities by deleting or reducing others. You cannot just continue to add bricks to peak-performing employees' little red wagons and expect them not to break! Their capabilities have limits, and if you are going to challenge them with new tasks, you must be willing to reassign some of their old ones. Reassigned tasks create a continuation of rotated responsibilities, which can be helpful in increasing the overall productivity of many employees in the organization. What is repetitious and boring to one is a new challenge to someone else!

Always be sensitive to the work demand of peak performers. Because they are so focused on high achievement and success, they may be reluctant to tell you when their plates are too full. Peak performers are driven to succeed, and may feel that if they acknowledge they are overloaded, they are admitting incompetence or failure. If this circumstance goes undetected, it can lead to potential burnout. Do not assume peak-performing employees will tell you when they have reached their limits. Many employees push themselves until they drop.

Align Authority and Responsibility.   As you keep your peak performers challenged by incrementally increasing their responsibilities, you should increase their authority accordingly. Unfortunately, in many organizations, responsibilities have shifted to employees, but managers still hold the authority to make decisions concerning those responsibilities. It is an all too common circumstance for peak-performing employees to be told by their managers, "This is your responsibility, but before you do anything, check with me first."

The misalignment of authority and responsibility is a major factor in causing peak-performing employees to leave organizations. Responsibility without authority increases stress and creates a formidable barrier to achievement. If your intention is to frustrate peak performers and drive them away, give them responsibility without authority. If it is your goal to keep them, align authority with new responsibilities.

Involvement in Decisionmaking

Peak-performing employees want to be included in decision-making. They want to have influence over their environments and they want to participate in decisions that affect their interests and responsibilities. Inclusion means participation. Peak-performing employees who are not included appropriately in the decisionmaking process or who perceive they have little or no influence will seek other opportunities where they can play a more significant role. Do not make them search elsewhere for inclusion and significance! The challenge in extending decisionmaking to your employees is the establishment of appropriate guidelines concerning their input. Although you may be willing to involve employees in decisions, there is a limit to their influence. Everyone must understand the boundaries to decisionmaking.

Decisionmaking Guidelines. Peak performers must understand expectations. Gray areas many times lead to misinterpretations, frustrations, and counterproductive behaviors. As a frontline manager, you must clarify the levels of employee influence. Your employees will participate appropriately if they understand the parameters of their inclusion. You must communicate

What is going to be done
Why it is going to be done
Who will perform specific tasks
When they must be accomplished

Whenever possible, include your employees in decisions of *how* those tasks and responsibilities are to be accomplished. *What*, *why*, *who*, and *when* is yours; *how* is theirs. Those are the boundaries in the culture of inclusion.

You cannot always involve your employees in all aspects of *how* things will be accomplished. Law, compliance, existing policies, ability requirements, and so forth, may mandate *how* something must be done. Many opportunities lend themselves to including employees in decisionmaking, however: Including your peak performers in determining how they can meet their goals and objectives invites them into the decisionmaking process at their greatest levels of expertise; it also allows you to tap their intellect and experience. When you include employees in decisions of *how*, you take a lot of pressure off yourself. You don't always have to be right; you can allow others to come up with the answers!

If you want peak performers to "buy in" to the organizational, group, team, or department's goals and objectives, give them influence over *how* they are going to be achieved. People tend to support decisions they help to make!

Please note that when someone is accused of being a "micro manager," one of that person's most flagrant behaviors is relentlessly controlling how things are done. Peak performers do not tolerate being micro managed.

Teach Decisionmaking Criteria.　Peak performers are capable of exercising common sense, of using good judgment, and of solving problems effectively. To participate successfully in making decisions, they must be prepared and trained in the decisionmaking process. They must learn the criteria used in making effective decisions. These criteria usually fluctuate and are different in various organizations and in differing circumstances. Unless you identify the factors that are most important to you and the organization in the decisionmaking process, peak performers may make decisions based on a different set of values and considerations.

They must understand the true mission of the department, group, team, and overall organization and your values and priorities if they are to make decisions consistent with those factors. Although some decisionmaking criteria remain stable, others may change depending on the situation. Peak-performing employees become frustrated if they do not understand the basis or foundation for decisions they are expected to make. They will seek other opportunities if they are consistently asked to make decisions without necessary information or complete understanding of all the factors involved.

Typically, the criteria for making decisions encompass time, quality, cost, and profitability.

Are the decisions you or others make in your organization consistently based on

- *Speed?* (the support of being the fastest provider of products and services in your industry)
- *Quality?* (in support of being the highest quality provider of products and services in your industry)
- *Cost?* (based on reducing costs and expenses in support of becoming the least expensive provider of products and services in your industry)
- *Profit?* (based on protecting the organization's profitable position in support of increasing shareholder value)

If peak performers believe that decisions are based on one set of factors, yet there is hidden criteria to be considered, they cannot possibly make effective choices. If they believe the quality of service drives decisions, they may make unacceptably high-cost decisions in attempts to achieve customer satisfaction. If you want them to make least-cost decisions, with quality considerations being secondary, they must understand your reasoning. If circumstances fluctuate, resulting in some factors situationally taking precedence over others, peak performers must be privy to the information that identifies these fluctuations. Peak performers cannot be expected to read your mind and instinctively know what to do. If they make decisions that are suddenly criticized because of changed criteria, their frustration will escalate and they may be reluctant to make decisions and expose themselves to future criticism.

Peak performers will seek other environments where clarity reigns. If you want peak performers to make decisions consistent with your thinking and the organization's thinking, they have to be in the loop.

Allow Peak Performers to Develop Others

The culture of inclusion incorporates opportunities and encourages peak performers to participate in the growth and development of others. Organizational mentoring programs are an excellent example. Once peak performers have established themselves within the organization, they can share their expertise with other employees who wish to attain greater success. Because it may not always be possible to provide managerial opportunities for peak performers in today's flattened, less hierarchical organizations, these employees can derive much satisfaction by influencing the achievements of others. Such opportunities also give peak performers additional avenues for learning the interactive skills necessary to influence others and a platform on which to showcase their developing abilities.

Peak performers can also be included in organizational training efforts. Who better to demonstrate the most effective way to perform a process or specific task than the people who do it well? There are disadvantages in allowing peak performers to train others; however, the good generally far outweighs the bad. Peak performers can be intimidating to those of lesser ability. Some people who do a job exceptionally well have trouble identifying with those who do not possess the same skills or willingness. Peak performers who are trained to be the trainer can do very well. Trained properly, they can have a tremendous influence on the productivity of individuals and the overall organization. Including them in the development and training of others provides positive outcomes at many levels.

The Culture of Change

Every organization is facing change at a rate unparalleled in economic history. The influence of technology, organizational restructuring, global competition, and customer expectations are just a few of the factors driving today's intense environment of continuous change. In the past, organizations changed at an evolutionary rate; today, the evolutionary pace has been obliterated by warp-speed revolutionary change.

You, your employees, and your organization cannot *not* change! One of the reasons you seek to find, hire, and keep peak-performing employees is to help accomplish the change mandates that you are facing. Peak performers are now hired to be change agents and to become the beacons leading others into tomorrow.

Peak performers and change present an interesting dichotomy. When first hired, peak performers champion change. In many cases, they see themselves spearheading change and establishing new processes, procedures, and outcomes. In the early stages of service, they demonstrate great flexibility and high willingness to make a difference. They often harshly judge the people around them who may be resisting change. Peak performers typically bring with them great enthusiasm for adopting new outlooks.

However, once peak performers become established within your organization and they assume positions of primacy as a result of their performance, leadership, and expertise, they, too, become entrenched in the current culture. They develop a stake in maintaining the status quo. Subsequent changes, perhaps mandated from the top of the organization or led by others, can threaten entrenched peak performers. It is not uncommon for individual peak-performing employees to exhibit intensely negative reactions to new change initiatives. After all, they may have the most to lose in a changed environment. For them, the current procedures and processes, which they may have championed, are working very well. Your peak performers are flourishing under the current circumstances. They have achieved stature through high performance. They have established themselves as number one. New change initiatives might relegate them to *number two*. For peak performers, change can be a threat to their current status.

Typically, once the wave of initial intense response has passed, peak performers again embrace change. They see themselves as capable and competent, and are confident they can continue to learn and succeed. Change becomes less threatening as they focus on their abilities to perform well. Their initial acute resistance tends to evolve into grudging acceptance, and then transforms into enthusiastic support.

How can you create the culture of change that will perhaps lessen the intensity of initial resistance, shorten the length of negative reaction, and prepare your employees to adopt change? How do you nullify the culture of resistance and nurture the culture of change? Here are some suggestions:

The Vision of Why

Peak performers support change if they understand the reasoning behind it. They are not necessarily good at supporting change just for the sake of change. They have to understand *why* it is happening. Attempting to push change without explanation only intensifies skepticism, resistance, and distrust. Because your peak performers are probably doing well under current conditions, change must be supported and legitimized through significant reason. Do not assume that your peak performers will automatically understand and embrace the change initiatives you present. They probably view the change from a completely different perspective.

In explaining *why*, it is important that you emphasize a "three-tiered" relevance of the change. Peak performers must understand why the change is being adopted from three separate vantage points:

- *Why* the change is in the individual peak performer's best interest
- *Why* the change is in the customer's best interest
- *Why* the change is in the organization's best interest

The more linkage you demonstrate between your change initiatives and these three tiers of relevancy, the greater the likelihood the change will be lightly resisted and positively supported. For peak performers, it is crucial that you help them understand how the change has positive ramifications for them.

Process Resistance Effectively

Resisting change is normal, and for peak performers resistance can initially be intense. Do not judge them harshly or imply that their resistance somehow reflects negatively on them. Because they struggle with change, it does *not* mean they aren't team players. Nor does it mean that they are inflexible or selfish. It merely reflects the need for time to process their reactions and to formulate positive responses.

Typically, the roots of change resistance fall into three categories. People resist change because they perceive

- Potential *loss*
- Pending *fear*
- Abuse or *unfairness*

Peak performers primarily root their resistance to change in visions of potential *loss*. Change presents the potential for the loss of many things, including position or status; access; planned growth and development; and comfort and familiarity. In creating and maintaining the culture of change, extend great effort through your words and actions to ensure that your peak performers receive the training and opportunity necessary to maintain their current top-performing status. Do not allow them to be left behind by the change. Be sure they experience no reduction in access to you, their boss, or other key people with whom they currently enjoy connection. One of the most important factors in successfully leading peak performers through change is to address and eliminate their perceptions of potential loss.

Future Focus

Peak performers take great pride in what they have accomplished. If change initiatives are presented as being critical of the past or a significant emphasis is placed on the necessity of change to fix past problems, peak performers predictably will rebel. If your change implicitly criticizes their past performances, they are quick to defend what they have done and take great offense to your implication that their past efforts have been less than stellar. Always position change initiatives as looking toward the future.

When you introduce change, emphasize that it is not because the past was bad, but because the future is different. Acknowledge your peak performers' past achievements and efforts, and then explain that the challenges facing the department, group, team, or organization are different now than ever before. Change is necessary to meet the new realities, not to fix the past. Peak performers are eager and highly motivated to face the future; do not force them into defending their past. Change is not an indictment of the yesterday; it is a positive statement of the difference of today and tomorrow.

Never Offer Invalid Assurances

A negative trap that lures many managers and organizations is to make assurances during the introduction of change that there really won't be much effect on the individual department, group, or team. Statements such as, "We're going to be doing things differently, but you won't see a whole lot of change. Don't worry. For the most part, everything will remain the same," are bogus and barefaced untruths! Trying to assure people that they will experience little disruption is a corruption of your change message. Lulling them into complacency merely delays and intensifies negative reactions. When changes do occur, they will probably feel as if you lied to them. Telling them they will experience little or no difference is dishonest. Will they be

- Asked to do more with less?

- Assigned new tasks and responsibilities?
- Experiencing restructuring, head-count reduction, and so forth?
- Experiencing new procedures and processes?

Of course!

Never make empty assurances during the change. Things will be different. That's why it's called change!

Align the Announcement and the Adoption

It is in everyone's best interest to announce pending change as early as possible. Let people know that change initiatives are on the horizon, and avoid intense, unnecessary surprises. The earlier you preannounce change, the more time you have to prepare your employees. At the time of announcement, however, you must establish and put in place realistic time lines for carrying out the changes. How many times have you gone to a meeting to discuss a pending change only to find that some of the elements were not in place? Statements such as, "We had hoped to have this ready for our meeting; however, we weren't able to do so" send enormously negative messages to your employees. They create a picture of disarray, unpreparedness, and even incompetence. Never announce change without being able to meet the announced time lines. If you announce in September that your employees will see new procedures and processes at the beginning of the new year, make that happen. Rather than alerting your employees to a change that you are not ready to adopt, you are better off delaying the announcement.

Peak performers will probably be ready to move ahead by the time the change is supposed to take place and they will be frustrated by your inability to keep your agreements.

Provide Summaries of Progress

Peak performers are interested in the relevance of change. Develop a consistent flow of information to keep employees apprised of the progress and success of change initiatives. Even if they are not enthusiastically supportive of the changes about to occur, they will probably energize their support when they see success. Develop change scoreboards. Create mechanisms to chart the results of change and communicate these outcomes to your employees. Even if the change does not meet initial expectations, you are better off identifying the reality, confronting it, and openly discussing it with your employees; if you don't, they will discuss it negatively among themselves. Visibly display the results through graphs, charts, and diagrams, and support the findings with as much data as possible to reinforce the culture of change.

The Culture of Celebration

As your organization experiences change and you are consistently imploring your employees to improve and to increase their efficiency and productivity, it is also important to create an environment in which success is celebrated incrementally. Peak performers recoil in anger and frustration if they feel they are being taken for granted or that no one is paying attention to their efforts, contributions, and outcomes. The culture of celebration honors employees' efforts and achievements in conjunction with the consistent elevation of standards and expectations.

If the drumbeat of the negative message tells employees over and over again that they must improve, they must get better, it is equivalent to telling them over and over again, "You're not good enough, you're not good enough, you're not good enough." Peak performers do not respond to a repeated negative message. Although they are driven to improve and consistently strive to increase their performances, they also want to be acknowledged for the contributions they are making. They are eager to improve; however, they want to hear that their performance isn't bad either. For peak performers, the demands for continuous change or continuous improvement, unaccompanied by celebration, become nothing more than continuous criticism. The culture of celebration creates a pipeline of positive messages to balance the ongoing appeals to improvement.

Positive Reinforcement

Peak performers want to be recognized for the individual, unique, contributing performers that they are. Although they do not necessarily need outside affirmations to define their own self-worth, they certainly want to hear the outside affirmations! They refuse to be taken for granted and develop extreme resentment when their performances and achievements go unnoticed. Failing to provide positive reinforcement to peak performers results in reduced longevity. If you do not appreciate their efforts, they will find someone who does.

How can you effectively provide positive reinforcement for peak performers? Your message must be specific. Do not deliver such general stroking messages as, "You're doing a good job, keep it up." Those messages are interpreted as insincere, and many peak performers believe they are being handled or manipulated if their managers deliver them consistently. Peak performers see specific positive reinforcement as sincere. Your messages must be targeted toward peak performers' specific actions, achievements, and behavior. A positive reinforcement message to peak performers should be structured like this:

"Keesha, that productivity report you turned in this morning was excellent. It is by far one of the best reports that I've ever read. You presented your results and ideas very well, and your summarization was excellent. I wanted you to know how much I appreciate your work."

This specific message tells your peak performers that you are aware of their work (you obviously read the report!) and you honor them as unique and individual performers. If peak performers know that you see them as just one of the herd, they react poorly. They want to be seen as high-performing individuals.

For frontline managers, there is another primary reason for using positive reinforcement with your peak performers. Positive recognition balances the delivery of constructive criticism, which is sometimes necessary. Peak performers do not like to hear their work criticized any more than anyone else; however, if criticism is communicated properly, they are usually willing to accept your comments if they are also receiving appropriate positive reinforcement. If the only comments they receive from you concerning their work are critical, they resent your lack of balance. They tune you out if you are predictably negative in your communication. If they are receiving appropriate recognition for their positive behaviors and performance, they are more likely to accept your criticisms as legitimate. You earn the right from the peak performers' perspective to critique their efforts legitimately if you are willing to acknowledge the abundance of their good contributions as well.

Group Celebrations

Although peak performers want to receive individual recognition, it is also important for them to be included in group celebrations. When the department, group, or team meets or exceeds goals, completes a project, or successfully accomplishes a change initiative, they should be honored collectively for their results. Celebrations may include group acknowledgement at a meeting that encourages the group to take a collective bow; providing lunch, donuts, bagels, and so forth, as an acknowledgement of their efforts (food is very celebratory!); or perhaps giving everyone a T-shirt celebrating their specific successes. Losing sight of the importance of individual and group celebration is a common, yet unfortunate, circumstance in many organizations today; it is one of the reasons some organizations are plagued by the defections of peak performers.

Why do some organizations have greater success in retaining peak performers than others? It is undoubtedly rooted in the development and nurturing of a culture of retention.

11

Managerial Strategies

Art Lucas of the Lucas Group:

All the surveys I've seen indicate that one of the primary reasons people leave jobs is not necessarily for money. It's generally because they don't feel appreciated enough. They don't feel that their manager or organization truly respects and values them for the contributions they make. Obviously, people leave for exceptional opportunities. If something comes along to really entice them, an exciting new challenge can cause them to leave. But most leave because they are not treated well. Some companies are difficult to recruit from because they do a good job in making their employees feel valued. Others are relatively easy to recruit from because they do not treat their employees well. As an example, and I don't want to be too self-congratulating here because there are many things we need to work on in our organization, and I have spent many sleepless nights thinking about how to continue to keep our key people. A recruiter called me a few months ago who specializes in placing people in the staffing industry. She told me she had been trying to recruit some of my managers and senior people for the last two years. She said she hadn't been able to get any of them to consider changing jobs. This led her to finally decide to try to make us her client and place people with us rather than trying to take them away. I asked her why she felt our people refused to leave. She said they truly feel loved and appreciated. While it sounds silly in today's workplace, it's very true. To retain people, there has to be a lot of organizational caring. People must know that you are really in their corner and you're trying, within reason, to work with them to develop their career, involve them, and to make them happy. You certainly have to share the wealth and pay them well. They also have to feel that they are with an organization that is a winning team and that there is a close comradeship within their environment. We work hard to create a culture where people really share information with each other, like each other, work together, play together. Many are probably friends outside of the office. It's an open environment versus an environment that is guarded, distrustful, secretive, etc. Those are the companies that are easiest to recruit from. Companies that are very open, where people really care about each other, and where there's generally a good feeling, are much more difficult to recruit from.

How do you create that environment? What are the most influential things you, as a frontline manager, can do to keep your valuable peak-performing employees? Here is a list of critical action points that will increase your retention. Some of these actions are unilateral and you can carry them out on your own; with others, you will need support. All will have an effect on keeping peak performers.

Will you have total managerial control of them all? Probably not. You can influence only what you have influence over. Use whatever influence you do have to make these action points a reality in your organization.

Make Tough Probationary Decisions

Earlier we stated that the best way to avoid problem employees is not to hire them. Probationary periods offer you an extended period to evaluate the quality of your hiring decisions. If you have made an error, discover it early. Cut your losses and find peak-performing replacements who are worth retaining! Carefully assess your new employees' performance and behavior patterns during their probationary period and be willing to sever your relationship if they do not meet your standards. Once you allow problem employees with marginal performance or disruptive behaviors to gain permanent status, your managerial challenges multiply at an explosive rate. Not only must you deal with them individually; they can disrupt the entire group, team, department, or organization.

Unfortunately, in many organizations today frontline managers have not identified the specific standards that probationary employees must meet if they are to achieve permanent status. Many new employees gain permanency merely by attendance. If you have a six-month probationary period and they show up on Day 181, surprise, surprise, they become permanent!

It is imperative that you develop a guideline for the skills and performance levels new employees must achieve during their probationary periods to allow them to attain permanency. Probationary periods exist to assess hiring decisions. Make sure you conduct effective assessments. If you have made a bad or marginal decision, admit it and take corrective action. Retention does not mean keeping marginal people.

Have you ever had employees who didn't perform well during probation but who got better? Perhaps anecdotally there has been one in a million; however, the odds are overwhelmingly against that happening! New employees are on their best behavior during probation.

Maintain Compensation

Art Lucas also cautioned: "You cannot have compensation plans based solely on your internal policies. You must have compensation plans based on market rates. You have to pay your people in the range that the market is dictating. If you do that and you are really good to your people, they are much more difficult to recruit and likely to stay long-term."

Survey your competitors and other organizations in your area that may potentially recruit your employees to ensure you maintain an awareness of current compensation rates. (Find out what the current market earnings are for people in your position as well!) Do not wait to discover that you are below market compensation rates by losing peak performers unexpectedly to others who are willing to pay them more. That's an expensive lesson.

Be proactive in gathering as much information as you can. You must maintain competitive compensation rates or you will become nothing more than a training ground for those organizations that do pay appropriately. They will let you hire, train, and develop people, and then come along and take the best and the brightest away from you! If is foolish to pay below market compensation yet continue to spend money recruiting to replace the employees you lose. You are paying either way; you may as well pay for performance! Unnecessary turnover is horribly expensive. For many peak performers, compensation is not the most important issue; however, it is always an issue. If you can't or won't pay peak performers, don't expect to keep them.

Maintain Accessibility to Adequate Resources

For peak performers to achieve to their greatest ability and continue doing so, they must have organizational resources available to sustain performance. These include accessibility to information, technology, equipment, and outside resources, as well as accessibility to you, their boss. Peak performers who know they are capable of doing better, yet realize their manager or their organization is reluctant to provide or grant them access to the necessary resources, begin to feel restrained or held back. They believe barriers are being placed in their paths unnecessarily or unfairly. They may assume the tasks and responsibilities for which they are being held accountable do not have a high organizational priority. How can you expect employees to be highly motivated and productive in the face of glaring signs that tell them they or their jobs are unimportant? Frustration with this lack of unavailability or unwillingness to provide the necessary resources frequently drives them away.

If resources are unavailable, you must communicate the facts to your peak performers (if you can't afford them, say so), and identify a realistic strategy or timetable for acquiring them. If peak performers see the absence of resources as a temporary condition, they will adapt. If they recognize it as long-term, they will leave.

Defeat Boredom

As previously discussed, boredom is a killer for peak performers. They must be continually challenged, and if they fall into a rut of ongoing, unchallenging, and repetitive tasks, performance and motivation decrease. Ultimately, they will either lapse into a coma or seek more stimulating opportunities. You, as a frontline manager, and the overall organization must continuously address the question, "How can we break up the boredom around here?" Not all boredom can be eliminated; however, search relentlessly for ways to wipe out as much of it as possible. Peak performers fall prey to an inherent boredom trap. They are good at what they do, and so they get more of it to do! Unless you also provide concurrent challenges, alternatives, or diversions, they can suffer mind-numbing boredom. Once a peak performer has mastered a task, no matter how complex, important, or challenging, the potential arises for repetition-based boredom to erupt.

You can counter boredom in many ways. Some were mentioned in Chapter 10: "Creating the Culture of Retention." The most successful include

- Training
- Mentoring of others
- Vacations and time off
- Assignment of new tasks
- Temporary assignments in support of other areas

Maintain constant vigilance for the signs of increasing levels of boredom. This is an issue over which frontline managers can exercise significant influence. When peak performers get bored, they're gone.

Increase Peak Performers' Visibility

Tom Trotter of Howmet Castings commented: "If I have an engineer who has done something outstanding, and my objective is to try to retain that employee at Howmet, I will give him or her as much exposure to upper management as I can. When a promotional opportunity comes up, either here or within another Howmet facility, that employee is well thought of and considered for the upward move."

Provide opportunities for your peak performers to increase their organizational visibility. Assign them significant roles in conducting or participating in meetings; allow them to train others; give them opportunities to present information to upper levels of management; and involve them in increased customer contacts. These are a few ways of increasing and maintaining their visibility. If peak performers see they are being pigeonholed or stuck off somewhere in a corner where nobody notices them, rapid discontent sets in. If they feel they have appropriate visibility and exposure to important contacts that may ultimately provide new career opportunities, their confidence increases and they embrace opportunities for continued service. Involvement in cross-functional problem-solving teams, visits to other organizational facilities, United Way campaign activity, and outreaches of community support are additional examples of opportunities for increased visibility. Peak performers want to be big fishes in the pond. Put the spotlight on them whenever possible.

Avoid Fear-Based Motivation

Peak performers are not motivated by fear! Threats and intimidation are not effective methods of motivation. Period! If you somehow threaten peak performers' jobs, they will save you the hassle of even writing up a warning. They will be gone! Peak performers are not concerned about what you can take away from them. They know they have other options. Highly creative, highly productive people are not motivated to great achievement by fear of bad things that could happen to them if they don't perform. Peak performers are motivated by gain. They are focused on what they *get* from their jobs, not what can be taken away. Gain equals job satisfaction. Although each peak performer defines job satisfaction differently, all would identify the common threads of being appreciated, feelings of self-accomplishment, being compensated fairly, and the knowledge that their work is important.

Fear-based management styles are obsolete. At best, they are counterproductive with peak performers, and at worst, they are destructive. Management styles that focus on empowerment, participation, and accomplishment by raising the gain for employees yield much greater results.

In my book, *The Bad Attitude Survival Guide: Essential Tools for Managers* (Addison Wesley, 1998), I deal with developing an effective, positive leadership style and avoiding the traits of fear-based, autocratic, and authoritarian management. I strongly recommend that you refer to that resource to assess your management style and study effective leadership alternatives.

A key question for all frontline managers to ask is this: "How can I increase the productivity and motivation of my people by raising the gain for them?"

Establish and Maintain Trust

Workplace trust is fragile. No matter what you do as a manager, you have no guarantee that your employees will trust you. Trust is easier to violate than to establish. Proving to people that you cannot be trusted is easier than encouraging them to trust you. The willingness to trust and the commitment of trust are also controlled by each individual's perceptions. People can see you as untrustworthy, whether there is a basis for that or not. Whether your peak performers trust you is up to them; all you can do is conduct yourself in a trustworthy manner and hope you earn their trust.

Unfortunately, with most peak performers, once you have violated their trust, you will rarely regain it. Under any circumstances, it takes significant time to rebuild trust. Time is something peak performers won't give you. When trust is violated, they are gone! You cannot rebuild trust with a ghost!

Some of the most critical factors in establishing trust are

Keep Your Agreements. Napoleon Bonaparte is reported to have said, "The best way to keep your word is never to give it." Words of great wisdom! You are better off saying nothing or saying *no* than creating agreements that you cannot or will not keep. Obviously, you keep your major agreements or you would not be employed as a frontline manager! Most frequently the broken agreements that erode trust are the result of minor commitments or unrealized expectations that have gone unfulfilled. Be careful always to keep your word and follow up on all of the commitments you make, regardless of how minor they appear to you. Do not tell peak performers that you will take care of something (no matter how insignificant) and not do so.

- If you promise to get them some information, *do it.*
- If you promise to fix a problem, *do it.*
- If you promise to check on something for them with someone else, *do it.*
- If you promise you will make an exception for them, *do it.*

Broken agreements result in broken trust. Trust erodes quickly. Peak performers need to know that they can count on their boss.

Maintain Confidentiality. Information given in confidence must never be shared with others. If peak performers discover that you have somehow violated their confidentiality, you will never regain their trust. Peak performers also react negatively to your sharing confidential information about others with them. Of course, they want to hear it. Most people are open to hearing rumors and gossip; however, they also assume that if you are willing to talk about someone else with them, you will be willing to talk about them with someone else. Inappropriately sharing confidential information does not create bonding with your peak performers; it merely proves to them that you cannot be trusted.

Confidentiality extends to past employees as well. Just because employees have left the organization, it does not mean that their rights to confidentiality have expired. Always protect confidential information. Take it to your grave.

As a frontline manager, proving through your consistent behavior that you can be trusted unquestionably with confidential information is critically important to you. Confidentiality enhances careers.

Never Usurp Credit. A major trust violator in today's workplace is taking inappropriate credit for someone else's ideas or accomplishments. When peak performers make suggestions or solve problems, be sure that they receive the appropriate credit. Never take credit for someone else's intellectual contributions or achievements.

As a frontline manager, you face an interesting challenge. When your department, group, or team performs well, you receive credit and recognition from those above you in the organization. You deserve it! You are responsible for the performance of your employees. When they do things well, you deserve to be recognized. It is also important, however, that you accept this credit and recognition appropriately by acknowledging the contributions of your employees. You achieve success in concert with them, not at their expense.

If you have ever had someone else take credit for your ideas or actions, you know how devastating that can be to trust.

Maintain Honesty. Never intentionally mislead or provide incorrect information to your peak performers. Being honest is telling the truth, as you know it to be. If you are not at liberty to share information, say so. Do not deny having the knowledge. Do not try to sugarcoat information. If you have bad news to deliver, do so honestly. Do not try to cover it up. Maintaining honesty also includes admitting your mistakes and acknowledging when you have behaved inappropriately.

Maintaining honesty does not mean that you will never be wrong or inaccurate in your statements. You may tell the truth as you know it only to find out later that you did not have all the available information or that your data was incorrect. When you find yourself in those circumstances, correct your statements as soon as possible. Acknowledge that you told the truth as you knew it at the time and now want to clarify your statements with additional information.

Communicate Effectively

Effective communication is the number one challenge facing every manager and organization in today's workplace. No matter how hard you try, no matter how good you are at communicating, there is always room for improvement. Peak performers experience high frustration in environments of poor communication. They want to know what is going on, and they do not respond well to being left in the dark.

Tom Trotter:

> The most difficult part of almost every task is communication. I find when people are well informed and there is a constant flow of both formal and informal communication, they tend to be happier employees and want to stay. If we get too busy to really focus on communication, we create people that don't know what

is going on and they have more questions than answers. If so, they have a tendency to look elsewhere for those answers, and I think that's natural. The most important thing is to maintain constant communication and doing whatever it takes to keep employees informed.

Here are some specific guidelines for increasing your communication effectiveness.

Share Information Equally.   Be sure that your peak performers acquire their information directly from you. In many organizations, information is used dysfunctionally to reward or punish people. The people in favor receive a constant flow of communication from management; those out of favor are denied information. This creates the "in-crowd" and "out-crowd." All peak performers want to believe that they are part of the "in-crowd." The in-crowd receives information directly from management. They get it from the horse's mouth. The out-crowd receives information through rumor, gossip, and the grapevine. Rumor, gossip, and the grapevine usually spread negative information that lowers productivity, morale, and works against management. Leaving peak performers out of the loop makes them dependent on the informal information highway!

To avoid misunderstandings, share information with everyone consistently, and if at all possible, at the same time. Do not share information with a few favored employees and expect them to disseminate it out to the rest of your employees. Distortions, whether intentional or unintentional, will happen, and some employees will end up receiving information that is inaccurate and unproductive. So much conflicting information is available to employees through other sources that employees must have confidence that their manager is giving them the truth.

What to Communicate. Knowing what to communicate is always a big part of the communication struggle. On one hand, you do not want to withhold valuable information from your employees unintentionally; on the other hand, you do not want to bury them under an avalanche of unimportant data. Everyone in today's workplace is suffering from information overload.

A general managerial guideline for evaluating the relevance of information is always to share with your employees information concerning

- Beginnings and endings
- Changes
- Developing needs
- Priorities and deadlines
- How current activities may have future effects

If you send a steady stream of information to your peak performers that addresses these five circumstances, you will keep them aware and up-to-date on the most meaningful information.

React to Problems When They Occur

One of the biggest complaints that peak performers have about their managers is that "they don't fix the problems around here." Although peak performers do not see themselves as part of the problem, they are quick to recognize the problems that occur in other areas and with other employees. Their observations that problems go unaddressed are not usually far from the truth. Many managers hesitate in dealing with problems, hoping that somehow, if enough time goes by, the problems will fix themselves.

Hesitancy or inactivity sends a negative message to peak performers. It indicates that you are willing to tolerate problems and do not really care whether other employees are performing. Peak performers have a difficult time maintaining their level of motivation, effort, and productivity in the long term if they see that others are being allowed to skate. Peak performers want to be the best of the best; however, they do not want to carry a heavier burden than is required of others. Significant problems due to perceptions of unfairness can erupt when some employees' poor performance or disruptive behavior is not addressed appropriately. This is a fight you do not want to pick with your top people.

When peak performers do make you aware of problems, establish their expectations of your reaction. Tell them that you appreciate their making you aware of the problem and commit to investigating it and taking whatever action that you determine is appropriate. Make them aware that just because they may not see visible action on your part, they should not assume that you have done nothing. In personnel matters especially, follow-up is confidential and should be invisible to others. Assure employees that you will act to guard confidentiality with others just as you would with them, and that they should soon see the problem corrected. They should not expect to see a visible action with the problem employee. Help those who notify you of a problem to understand that just because they do not see overt action on your part, they should not assume nothing is being done.

Conduct Timely Performance Appraisals

If you want to aggravate peak-performing employees intentionally, delay their performance appraisals. It is usually not a wise idea to try to aggravate these employees, but if you really want to do it, this is a great way!

Peak performers relish the opportunity to discuss their results and their plans for future growth and development. They look forward to appraisal sessions. If you schedule performance appraisals for employees' anniversary dates, be sure that you are prepared to conduct your meeting within one week of the date. If you make all your appraisals at one time, perhaps at the beginning of the year, if at all possible, schedule your peak performers first. They want the information and are frustrated when it is not forthcoming. If they think you are delaying their performance appraisals, significant resentment results; they probably conclude that you are procrastinating to avoid increasing their compensation or because you do not consider them, or meeting with them, important. Delayed performance appraisals tend to reinforce perceptions of being taken for granted, and peak performers interpret that as a sign from heaven that it is time for a move. Appraisals not held on a timely basis are unkept agreements that erode trust.

Also, conduct performance appraisals effectively. Do not treat them as if they are unimportant, and do not appear to be unprepared. Your peak performers will be prepared, and they will take offense if you do not demonstrate the same level of commitment.

Performance appraisals are a valuable management tool in retaining peak performers. Use them wisely.

Treat Peak Performers with Dignity and Respect

Peak performers demand to be treated with great dignity and respect. Many people believe that dignity and respect are eroding in today's society, but peak-performing employees will settle for nothing less than respect in the workplace. Although you would never intentionally treat peak performers with lack of dignity or respect, the reality is, everyone sends those negative messages to others without realizing it. Whether intentional or not, treating someone disrespectfully signals personal disregard and lack of value. No peak performers flourish in that environment, nor do they choose to stay and subject themselves to further mistreatment.

The list of negative managerial behaviors that contribute to perceptions of lack of dignity or respect is long. Here are three to be avoided at all costs.

Abrasive or Abusive Conduct. This is a huge umbrella that covers many negative managerial behaviors, but the most frequently occurring are

- Temper tantrums
- Shooting the messenger
- Inappropriate jokes and humor
- Negative nonverbal communication
- Inappropriate analogies and references

Although there are exceptions, a common thread of abrasive or abusive conduct is subjecting someone to public embarrassment. When an employee is made to look bad in front of others, it is considered abrasive, abusive, and inappropriate managerial behavior. When it is appropriate to criticize someone, do so in private. Never make anyone an example by exposing or subjecting that person to ridicule in the presence of others. Publicly embarrass peak performers and you may never see them again.

Talking Behind Someone's Back. Never talk about employees behind their backs. Never say anything about someone that you would not say directly to that person. You have probably had the experience of learning that someone from whom you expected better behavior participated in criticizing you when you were not there to explain yourself or was unwilling to defend you when others may have been critical. Your reaction typically would include anger, feelings of betrayal, and deep hurt. Just as you do not want others to do this to you, be sure that you do not do it to them. Talking about others behind their backs is an attempt to make yourself look better at their expense. Not only is it cowardly behavior, it is one of the most disrespectful things you can do. Unfortunately, denigration of the workforce is a significant problem for many managers in today's workplace. Usually the people talked about are those not liked. You do not have to like your peak performers, but it does not give you the right to be abrasive, abusive, or disrespectful.

Failing to Listen.   Listening to an employee is one of the most respectful things you can do. As previously discussed, it sends messages of great value and affirmation. It demonstrates that you honor that person's intellect and consider the employee worth your attention. Failing to listen to someone sends the horribly disrespectful message of low value. Unfortunately, listening is one of the least practiced managerial skills in today's workplace. Most frontline managers fall into the trap of not listening appropriately because of demands on their time. Often you do not have time, in many cases, to do an effective job of listening. In reality, you cannot afford to not take the time to listen; it is one of the primary things that managers must do differently in today's workplace. As previously discussed, when peak performers perceive they are not being listened to, they yearn to find an environment in which they will be more highly valued.

Retaining peak performers is one of the most important responsibilities you have. Some factors causing turnover are beyond your control, but many offer great opportunities of influence. To be successful takes commitment and a willingness on your part to change. Today's frontline manager must do things differently.

Retention Assessment	**Yes**	**No**
Do you		

1. Offer continuous training to employees? ___ ___
2. Delegate to employees' strengths? ___ ___
3. Listen to employees? ___ ___
4. Provide incremental increases of responsibilities to employees? ___ ___
5. Involve employees in the decisionmaking process? ___ ___
6. Have organizational mentoring programs available for employee participation? ___ ___
7. Help employees adapt to change initiatives through the use of explanations and "why" information? ___ ___
8. Provide access to you, the boss, during the change process to address employees' perceptions of "loss?" ___ ___
9. Ensure that change initiatives focus on the organization's future, not on employees' past performances? ___ ___
10. Keep employees informed about the progress and success of the change? ___ ___
11. Make tough probationary decisions? ___ ___
12. Maintain compensation in a range the market is dictating? ___ ___

13. Provide access to the necessary resources for sustaining employees' peak performances? ___ ___

14. Offer accessibility to you, their boss, as a resource? ___ ___

15. Counter employees' boredom by "creating the culture of retention?" ___ ___

16. Provide opportunities for employees to increase their organizational visibility? ___ ___

17. Avoid fear-based motivation techniques? ___ ___

18. Establish and maintain trust in the workplace? ___ ___

19. Communicate effectively? ___ ___

20. React to problems on a timely basis? ___ ___

21. Conduct timely performance appraisals? ___ ___

22. Treat all employees with dignity and respect? ___ ___

23. Celebrate the successes achieved throughout the change process? ___ ___

24. Provide specific positive reinforcement to your employees? ___ ___

25. Conduct regular team and group celebrations of success? ___ ___

No responses indicate opportunities for growth and development.

12

In Summary

Without a doubt, responsibilities of finding, hiring, and keeping peak performers are among the most important challenges facing every frontline manager in today's workplace. You are considered an effective manager if your people are productive. The only way to achieve that is to hire productive people. You position yourself for promotion when you are able to increase the efficiency and productivity of others effectively. You position yourself for promotion by hiring employees who are capable of increased efficiency and productivity and who are willing to learn. It's been said that when the student is ready, the teacher will appear. You can guide your employees through the learning process if they are willing students.

One of the biggest impediments to overall productivity is the disruptive behavior of problem employees. The best way to avoid problems is not to hire them. The biggest influence on your current productivity and future growth and development is the quality of the people you employ. The best managers in the world cannot achieve great levels of success unless they hire peak-performing people.

This book has shown you some specific strategies and techniques that will enable you to increase your hiring effectiveness. The key question now is whether you are willing to use these strategies and techniques, practice repetitiously to increase your proficiency, and apply them to your hiring challenges. Only you can make that commitment.

You have also discovered the significant actions that you and your organization must take to retain the peak-performing employees you hire. Finding and hiring the best is only a part of the process; you have to develop and keep them as well. Is there anything more heartbreaking to managers than finding and hiring exceptional employees, only to see them drift away? Not all turnovers can be eliminated, yet you can extend longevity and you can address many of the factors that are driving the best away.

In a perfect world, you could do everything necessary to keep peak performers. In the real world, you can't. Your influence may be limited and the resources that are necessary to keep peak performers may not be available within your organization. Perhaps you cannot overcome the existing barriers that drive employees away. In reality, you may have little influence over retention. Use whatever level of influence you do have. Encourage upper-level management to consider the changes necessary to improve retention. Carry out the actions that you can control unilaterally. Do everything within your sphere of influence to keep your peak performers.

The ten most significant reasons peak performers leave their current organizations are (*not* in order of importance or priority)

- Feeling unappreciated/being taken for granted
- Boredom: repetition, repetition, repetition
- Misalignment of authority and responsibility
- Poor communication
- Not being listened to

- Lack of involvement in the decisionmaking process
- Submarket compensation
- Unclear goals, objectives, and expectations
- Absence of positive recognition
- Poor management

Assess the potential for these factors to drive your peak performers away and do whatever is possible to minimize their effects.

The challenge is yours. I hope you have found this book helpful.

In closing, I think it is appropriate to share some final comments from Tom Trotter of Howmet Castings.

I think it's important to underscore the importance of individual frontline managers taking ownership for their recruiting and retention. Unfortunately, it's something that we have taken for granted for a long time. We can't continue to do that. It has to be one of our core management competencies, just like leading the business has got to be. It can't be something that we delegate. It's too important, and many times delegating this responsibility just doesn't work. In the long run, we're not going to have the right kind of people in our business if we don't take personal responsibility but we leave the tasks to others.

Index

About the Author

Harry E. Chambers, president of the Atlanta-based training and consulting group, Trinity Solutions, Inc., is an internationally known performance improvement specialist who works with organizations committed to improving the productivity of their managers and staff. Mr. Chambers specializes in leadership development, diagnosing and correcting performance problems, increasing communication effectiveness, and dealing with people who demonstrate poor attitudes and negativity.

With a reputation for providing content-rich programs that focus on delivering real-world strategies and techniques, he has earned a client list that includes United Technologies, the Marriott Corporation, *Inc. Magazine*, the Make-a-Wish Foundation, and the International Brotherhood of Electrical Workers.

He, his wife, Christine, and son, Patrick, live in the Atlanta suburb of Peachtree City and a in cabin in the north Georgia mountains.

For more information, please contact Harry E. Chambers and Trinity Solutions, Inc., at 1–800–368–1202.

E-mail: trinitysol@aol.com

Web: www.trinitysol.com